Where Regret
Cannot Find Me

For
Kayy —
Knowing your path
is filled with
great love!
All the
best,
David

Where Regret Cannot Find Me

Essays from the Spiritual Path

By David Ault

To order additional copies of this book, contact:
Xlibris Corporation
1-888-7-XLIBRIS
www.Xlibris.com
Orders@Xlibris.com

For Karen and Eddie:

Whose unconditional hearts and patient ears have helped me through this entire process. I am blessed by your love and touched by your friendship. Thank you for being my lids.

For Kevin:

Whose decision was the catalyst for the beginning of these writings. Thank you for playing your part. May that place over the rainbow find its way to you.

Contents

Where Regret Cannot Find Me

I have a crack in my windshield. Somehow a single pebble escaped the suction of the fresh asphalt on the Interstate by my house in Los Angeles and launched itself towards the glass of my truck. What started as a single bullet shaped scar soon gave way to a free flowing line that worked its way across the glass like the outline of the surrounding Southern California Mountains. It wasn't the first time that this cosmetic "flaw" had paid a visit. With a modicum of regularity, it seemed that every car I'd ever owned eventually displayed this. Yet, this time, there wasn't the urgency to have it fixed. I even stopped apologizing for it whenever I had a guest passenger. This thin, prism-like crack, with its peaks and valleys, became both mirror and messenger to my aching heart.

"Stop trying to cover me up," it seemed to lament. "Don't be in such a hurry to replace or fix me. So what if I'm not

1

perfect. Let me be your teacher."

My imperfect windshield and I made our way to a lunch with one of my oldest friends. Hope and I first met in sixth grade and bonded through our love of journalism and theatre. We stayed best buds from high school graduation through our years of living in New York City and Los Angeles. Yet, even though we lived only fifteen minutes apart now, there were times when our schedules were just crazy enough to keep us from seeing each other. This lunch was our new commitment to at least make the effort once a month to sit down to a meal together and catch up.

She called before to let me know that her four-year-old daughter, Sophia, would be joining us.

Sophia was at that stage of independent exploration where she insisted on dressing herself. Greens with purples, stripes with plaids, and in this case a black feather boa. Hope wanted to warn me ahead of time.

"How brave," I laughed, "I would never consider a boa in daylight."

There really wasn't much "catching up", as Sophia innocently demanded much of her mother's attention. Even with a bag full of distractions from books to games to dolls, she still wanted to be a part of our discussion. I marveled at what Hope had assembled to keep her daughter entertained, finding myself mentally reciting a phrase that was quick to age me.

"In my day…" Well, at least I hadn't ventured into the time segregating commentary about the number of miles I had to walk to school, I reasoned.

The established toy choices available to me at that age were Hot Wheels and G I Joes. If fortune smiled, an Etch-A-Sketch was thrown in—a far cry from the electronic, high tech gadgetry that blankets today's shelves.

Mine was a generation that played games outdoors. In the neighborhood of my adolescence, it was not uncommon, as the sun went down, for our mothers to be calling and calling. With sweat from the sweltering humidity as layer number one, dirt and pine sap nestled into the creases of our necks, arms and knees creating a zebra effect. We were hard pressed to give up tree climbing, fort building and the multiple uses of spare tires. However, the most popular game by far was always Hide and Seek. There were myriads of places to hide—under the house, in drainage ditch openings, in trees and on rooftops. As I became a seasoned Hide and Seek professional, I realized that I would much rather be the one who was "it". Hiding became boring fast and I always drew attention to myself so that I could be found. Being the seeker meant freedom to explore and search, and at those times when I felt exceptionally mischievous, I'd go inside and make a peanut butter and jelly sandwich while the others hid.

In retrospect, I can appreciate the parallel of that game with my spiritual path. There is that part of us that abhors hiding. To deny any part of the full spectrum of life—the disappointments as well as the victories, grief and joy, times of doubt as well as faith—is to hide from our feeling nature.

Now, the message of the windshield seemed vitally clear. Stop judging how you feel.

3

I was experiencing the mental exhaustion that comes from standing in front of the dam of disappointments. Pressing my hands against the cracks to keep the regrets and sorrow at bay, I expended great amounts of energy in the denial of feeling, all the while rationalizing that I was doing the admirable thing.

I knew now I'd reached the point on my life path where I could no longer hold up the dam. It was time to let the walls crack, crumble and fall.

Days later, staring again at my fractured, yet freshly washed "illustration", I began to weep. You know, the sobbing kind. Yes, if you look back at the cover it will confirm that I am a man. It isn't that men don't cry, it's that men don't seem to cry very neatly. And this was one that had waited for 42 years to hit shore, an uninterrupted current that was extremely messy, spilling without tissue, Starbuck's napkin or moist towelette in sight. I had just started the drive from Los Angeles to Napa and was resolved to get to the wedding rehearsal I was officiating by early evening. But the tears had started free of even radio sad song stimulus. I could no longer hold it in.

The romantic break up from someone I loved dearly followed a litany of failed occurrences that seemed to plague my life in that past year. Everything I touched did not turn to gold; instead, it resembled mold.

Feeling like some cosmic delete button was eliminating everything I planned both personally and professionally, the waves of disappointment were crashing in on me like the hurricane surf I had watched as a child. Somehow the turbulent Gulf of Mexico seemed mild compared to this.

Honestly, I don't remember driving the six plus hours or the fact that I must have stopped for gas. I remember only the overwhelming grief that propelled the release. Anyone passing me on Interstate 5 in California who looked my way must have gotten an eye full.

These heartbreaking sobs were not just about the sadness of the relationship changing form. That was merely the catalyst. These tears seemed laden with the death of my father, the loss of so many friends and colleagues from AIDS, the struggles from my show business years, family issues, financial pit falls—even pimples in high school.

All I remember is that I allowed myself, once and for all, to be held by the arms of sorrow.

I'm not sure why I was always so apprehensive to venture into her arms or, when there, wish to wriggle my way out like a hug from an over-perfumed aunt.

I flashed onto a scene from the movie version of A Chorus Line. The director asks one girl after reviewing her resume', why she hadn't worked in over a year. You could tell by her face that she was searching her mental index to come up with an appropriate or appealing response. Instead she told the truth. "I had a nervous breakdown," she softly confesses, "I started crying one day and I couldn't stop."

I thought that would happen to me. If I tossed out that emotional line I might never be able to reel it back in. Experience has taught me my fears were unfounded.

Months afterwards, I attended a reception to honor a publisher in the field of metaphysics. It was held at an ex-

5

clusive hotel in Los Angeles in one of their finest banquet rooms. There was a sit down dinner with several introductions of visiting dignitaries and a congratulatory speech from a well-known author preceding the honoree. During the opening remarks, loud band music began to filter in from a wedding being held in the adjacent hall. The music was distracting and it was difficult even to hear what was being said about the publisher. Yet, no one said anything about it and the speakers kept plowing through their part of the program. Finally, when the honoree took his place behind the podium, he joked, "I've been excited about receiving this award for months but I didn't know it would come with a rendition of *Love Shack* by the B-52s. The tension relaxed, and the entire banquet hall exploded with laughter.

Just as the speaker finally acknowledged the "white elephant" in that room, releasing the tension, so does acknowledging sorrow. We then begin the move towards healing it. Denying it seems as useful as a Band-Aid over a gaping wound. It's better to let the wound be looked at, washed and salved.

Deepak Chopra wrote, "Pretending they (regrets) are not there is accepting the idea that they are somehow unhealable, unforgivable. Our greatest insight is that everything is all right. Our greatest delusion is we have made unforgivable mistakes."

However, the reverse of this acknowledgment reveals those who are "professionals" in being the walking wounded. They collect their victim charms and wear them on ID bracelets, shaking them in our faces. What would they talk about if they worked towards resolution? To me, that is stagnation, making a mantra out of "ain't it awful". What I'm referring to is simply acknowledging the regrets and taking actions to heal and cleanse them from becoming our identifiable calling cards.

Allowing our feeling nature free reign to express deepens our ability of understanding and strengthens our compassion.

As Ralph Waldo Emerson said, "Sorrow makes us all children again, destroys all differences of intellect. The wisest knows nothing."

I arrived in Napa, the front of my shirt soaked from tears and the accompanying runny nose. I quickly changed, wiped my face as best I could and approached the door to the wedding rehearsal. The bride flung open the door, took one look at me and said, "You look so peaceful. Thank God! We're all nervous wrecks!"

My first thought was, "If you only knew."

After the festivities, I spent some time walking around Napa. I love the area and I strolled from shop to shop stopping at my favorite used bookstore. At that moment I remembered a phone call I was to make and opened my day planner to find the number. The calendar section stared back at me and in the squares for the present weekend was written my partner's name and mine.

More tears.

Even in one of my favorite places, I couldn't seem to escape regret and sorrow. I remember thinking, "I just want to go somewhere where regret cannot find me."

I looked up at the bookstore window and realized I had found the title for my book.

It encompassed the great paradox, for in order to discover such a place we must first let it find us and invite it in, acknowledge its meaningful but temporary visit, creating the healing ability to move on. Just as in Hide and Seek, it felt better to be found.

The thirteenth century Sufi poet Rumi wrote:

> *This being human is a guesthouse.*
> *Every morning a new arrival.*
>
> *A joy, a depression, a meanness,*
> *some momentary awareness comes*
> *as an unexpected visitor.*
>
> *Welcome and entertain them all!*
> *Even if they're a crowd of sorrows,*
> *who violently sweep your house*
> *empty of its furniture,*
> *still, treat each guest honorably.*
> *She may be clearing you out*
> *for some new delight.*
>
> *The dark thought, the shame, the malice,*
> *Meet them at the door laughing*
> *And invite them in.*

Be grateful for whoever comes,
because each has been sent
as a guide from beyond.[1]

Opening the door to sorrow revealed a lady of sweet understanding. The depths of her compassion are comparative to God's own. She is the mistress who accompanies everyone in secret but longs to stroll side by side even in the light of day. Her beauty and vulnerable gifts are never fully appreciated unless they are brought into that light. It is the divine paradox of sadness and joy, dark and light, tears and laughter that turn our inward dial of life to the setting called "full experience". With senses so heightened we cry in the light and watch as our tears cascade and collect into pools of diamonds reflecting the rainbows of our souls.

The great Harlem Renaissance author Zora Neale Hurston once wrote, "I have been in sorrow's kitchen and licked out all the pots. I have stood on the mountain wrapped in rainbows, with a harp and sword in my hands."

Beginning to explore this new mountain, my hands held on to vulnerability and courage as supportive companions.

Now that sorrow was here, I no longer feared her for she had whispered to me that her arms were inviting. I had to agree. No longer was I focused on the energy of keeping my hands pressed against the cracks of the dam. I had freed them, watched it collapse and began floating in the collected tears of my lifetime. I no longer became concerned about when I'd stop or who could see, because sorrow now stroked

9

my hair, cradled me and rocked me through the night like the Eternal Mother.

The biblical metaphor reminds us we cannot put new wine into old skins. My prayers to be a bright light in a darkening world seemed attainable, for this metamorphosis delivered more compassion and clarity than I had ever known. I could feel, at last, new growth forming for my highest purpose to find its home.

The windshield still maintains its elongated crack. For now, it represents a map of an illuminating journey. I thank sorrow for that. As she leaves to make room for joy, she softly kisses me and I know that we will meet again.

1) What fears/judgments do you possess about entertaining the presence of sorrow? Are you willing to trust that by allowing yourself to explore these feelings, you will move through the experience and come to a place of peace?

2) In medieval legends, the knight realizes he must face his fear and turns toward his fire-breathing challenger, the dragon. By facing it, the knight can detect where it is vulnerable and weak and wields his sword toward the creature's demise. Ignoring or running from our regrets fuels their fire-breathing power as they scorch our happiness and detain us from our growth. Are you willing to turn and face your regrets and sorrows—to use your sword of worthiness and cut their stagnant ties to your well being? If not, can you define the "why" in your hesitation?

3) What's the worst thing that could happen if you did surrender to the sorrow? What's the best?

The Lid

Sitting on the well-manicured lawn, my bare feet flexed and stretched in their open-aired freedom as I enjoyed a bit of time travel. The morning sun carried me back to an age in my home of Beaumont, Texas when it was far more common to have exposed feet than crammed into Buster Brown church shoes or the cheapest pair of school sneakers my mother could afford. Now as I sat at the Huntington Gardens in Pasadena, California, the St. Augustine seemed filled with memory. The gardens, barely half an hour from my house, are a favorite local oasis. I'm still uncertain what I love most about the place; its sprawling, serene landscaping, libraries and galleries or the fact that they actually encourage you to walk on the grass.

With shoes and socks off, my toes played pick-up sticks with the individual blades of turf that embroidered a blan-

13

ket of green. I didn't care about "stubborn" chlorophyll stains on my jeans. I just needed to sit and stare at the flowers that were returning with spring. I envied the weightlessness of the butterflies that darted among the blossoms, wishing the morning breeze could lift me to join them in duet with the white-crowned sparrow.

My languishing thoughts were soon interrupted by a handful of people who were dutifully following a flora and fauna expert. I couldn't tell if the white-haired, khaki-wearing gentleman providing the commentary was a docent with the Huntington or, if the party of five were bridge playing friends who abandoned their cards because it was such a gorgeous day.

The man directing the group pointed out the grandest blossoms and matched them with the lingering fragrances.

"But even with their beauty," he said, "notice the foliage that surrounds them—the non-blooming, non fragrant varieties. These are what landscapers call "lids". Alone, they aren't as visually impactful but, when added with the more showy plants, they help create a greater, balanced aesthetic picture."

I smiled what I call a soul smile—a grin filled with so much gratitude for goose-bump synchronicity that it travels from face to heart. I was guided here. I sat captivated by nature's performance, the spring breeze dusting off the layered weariness of my heart and mind that came from using work as the vehicle for avoiding personal feelings. An unfamiliar vulnerability always surfaced when voluntarily dissolving into rest. It was easier to let old patterns of activity

14

kick into high gear. Why risk exploring all those unvisited emotions when there's so much "work" to do? Staying busy was a familiar repellent in warding off the stings of a lifetime of personal disappointment.

The imbalance played itself out earlier that same morning as the pre-dawn light lasered through my kitchen window.

Standing at the counter, I realized that a blender isn't much good without a lid.

With gummy globs of protein shake moisturizing my hair, tee shirt, cabinets and floor, I realized the simple act of putting the lid on the blender escaped me.

There was the short expletive at my carelessness and then the momentary look of stern consternation at the lid resting on the counter.

"Couldn't you have just floated up there and done your job without me? Didn't you know I was about to press the whirl button?"

But it was silly to blame the lid. Like those times when you drive and have no concrete recollection just how you got there, I was the one who veered into the unconscious lane.

I know I am not unique when it comes to tattooing a *rolling stone gathers no moss* across my psyche. But, that stone of "productivity" was pulverizing the metaphoric roses I was supposed to be taking the time to smell.

After some time with the quicker-picker-upper paper towels, I knew it was a day for the gardens.

Driving, I mulled over the morning's shenanigans and

15

marveled at this self-created cosmic parable that seemed to be revealing another life lesson.

All that any of us ever want in life is for someone to be our "lid." Not to suppress or judge our spectrum of emotions or even to come along and "fix it" but to simply provide a safe space when life's experiences sometimes press the liquefy button. Those human lids are our circle of friends, that sacred collection of individuals that remember who we really are and steadfastly love us, despite momentary (or even lengthy) lapses of judgment, pity parties or careless erring. When we doubt ourselves, they never do. When situations intensify and our lives seem grated, frappe'd and chopped, these lids seem to be there for the duration.

Wayne Muller, author, minister and therapist once told the story of his friend Helen and her son Jake. Jake was hyperactive. His energy would sometimes erupt in out-of-control acts that disrupted classrooms, his family and even his own well being. Like many parents, Helen had tried a variety of prescription drugs and other treatments but with little success.

Finally, out of desperation, Helen decided that every time Jake became hyperactive, she would grab him and hold him tightly on her lap. She wrapped her arms around her son, holding him so that he could hear her heartbeat. She did this, she said, so that he would quiet down enough to remember who he was.[2]

Muller revealed that within a few months, Jake's symptoms had subsided almost completely.

Helen was Jake's lid. Her capacity to see Jake for the

miracle he was, despite the outbursts, reveals the type of inner vision we all long to experience and achieve.

Now, sitting on the lawn, I invited mother earth to wrap her arms around me. Maybe, just maybe, if I quieted down enough, I could hear her heartbeat and remember.

As I wiggled my toes deeper in the cool grass, I watched the group move down the path and looked back to where they stood. I wanted to see for myself what a landscaping lid looked like. The man speaking obviously knew what he was talking about. Surrounding the ranunculus, blooming lavender, foxglove and Mexican sage were border grasses and plants that were somewhat nondescript yet important in the overall landscape. They did set the stage for the more vibrant plants to shine.

The movie, Billy Elliot, tells the story of a young boy unable to suppress his desire for dance despite his working-class father's disapproval. I was emotionally moved by the relationship between the dance teacher and Billy. This teacher, an older woman, would never have the accolades, public praise or celebrity that may once have filled her younger desires, but her vision and dedication to young Billy's chances helped guide him to see his dreams realized. Even when Billy scoffed, emotionally withdrew and lashed out at her, she never wavered. She was his lid.

As I write this, I'm traveling back to my hometown to deliver the eulogy for my sister Becky's memorial.

After nearly 30 years of struggle with multiple sclerosis, she let go of this earthly body, and perhaps in the here-after is feeling what it's like to walk, run, and dance again. I share the relief that my family feels in knowing that she no longer is suffering, yet still grieve for the sister that once was. Thirteen years older than me, Becky was the one who helped rear me after the death of my father. She bought my clothes, gave me those embarrassing summer crewcuts, took me to my first day of school, and drove the family to church every Sunday. Becky was naturally outgoing with a knack for remembering and telling the latest jokes and stories. Out of over 450 students in her senior class she was voted "the wittiest" with a reputation as the indomitable class clown. Even disease couldn't seem to diminish a punch line.

Nearly every day after school, I went to Becky and her husband's house to help out with housekeeping and yard work. Mostly, it was to help her get to the toilet. It would be awhile before she was hooked up full time to a catheter and a day nurse employed for her care. During my early high school years, she was still able to sit upright but struggled in pulling her body weight to a standing position with the walker. Even more challenging was maneuvering her body and the walker through the narrow bathroom door. The so-lution—find a way to carry her. Reminiscent of that Carol Burnett skit with the old couple in their rocking chairs pre-paring to stand up by shouting, "Get me started," Becky, facing me, would grip her hands around my neck counting off to three before attempting lift off. What always followed was material for those hidden camera shows. Standing like exhausted marathon dancers, I walked backwards dragging her towards the bathroom. Within that short distance, she would tell a joke to try and make me laugh. More often than not, it worked and her cornball humor would send us both falling to the floor.

"Knock, knock."

"Who's there?"

"Duane."

"Duane, who?"

"Duane the bathtub, I'm dwowning."

Then, she'd laugh so hard at her own delivery that you couldn't help but laugh back, even after hearing it a hundred times.

"Stop!" I'd gasp, but it was often too late, and she'd wet herself amid our giggling. Once, sprawled out on the shag carpet, she looked at me soberly and said, "I have to keep you laughing. It's the only way I feel I can contribute—the only way I can still be your big sister."

I could feel the ache in my heart as distinct as if someone had shot me.

"You'll always be my big sister," I softly said, facing her on the floor.

It was her way of revealing her feelings about how helpless and alone she felt. This comedic routine helped her forget, albeit momentarily, that she was disabled. Becky thought her role as my lid was over. She needed to know it never stopped.

My dear friend Karen tells the story of swimming competitively as part of a relay team across the English Channel. "In the water," she revealed, "you cannot see any sign of land. Your only lifeline is a funky old fishing boat that putters along side you. The boat operator counts your strokes, keeps an eye out for oncoming freighters, knows the tides and charts your course. They are there to feed you fresh water through a straw and encourage you to keep going."

How many times have we felt alone, swimming through life without direction—unable to see anything but the problem in front of us? Sort of like playing on a team of one without a spectator or cheerleader in sight. I thought of my sister, seemingly floundering in the murky waters of disease all those years. Yet, even at the end, with only eyes for communication, she was still trying to entertain the nurses, doctors and family. Once a lid—always a lid. She still wanted to be the support system, the boat operator—somehow wanting to lift herself and humanity out of its loneliness.

In this past year, a half dozen friends and congregants shared with me recent cancer diagnosis. As we sat, prayed, cried, and talked about it, all of them came to the conclusion that it wasn't the diagnosis that scared them—it was how they were going to pay for it. Even some with medical insurance knew that it was still going to generate major out-of-pocket expense.

I could relate. As I lay in the office of a Beverly Hills Ear Nose and Throat specialist this past year, I experienced the same concern. An eighteen-month cough had become so debilitating that I was blacking out and unable to keep food down. Months of tests, tissue samples and various medicines proved unsuccessful in discovering a solution. Because my first biopsy came back inconclusive, I returned a second time for another tissue sample. Before the procedure, the doctor nonchalantly whispered, "Looks like cancer, my friend."

I drove home, not obsessing about his comment, but wondering what I should begin selling if this were to be my next adventure.

Thankfully, my results were benign and alternative therapies led to a full recovery. But listening to these souls share their stories transported me back to that unforgettable ride home.

During the endless barrage of tests, MRI's, cat-scans and combined nontraditional modalities, I felt like I had stumbled into quicksand. With each dead-end, my spirit sank a little deeper. Now, as I listened to these people share their concerns, I could sense that they, too, felt they were sinking. It was inappropriate for me to stand on terra firma, as they sank, and say "Think positive!" And as powerful as affirmative prayer is, I've come to believe that our consciousness extends far beyond reciting words; I believe that supportive action is the mortar to rebuilding our faith. What these people needed was a stick, a hand, something to help pull them out from their bottomless worry.

From that the premise for *The Samaritan Project* was born. Our church set up a fund and began accepting donations through private contributions and fund-raising efforts, helping members in our spiritual family going through crisis. Mother Teresa often said, "We cannot all do great things,

21

but we can do small things with great love." These chari-
table acts, whether buying food, paying for a prescription
or medical insurance or other necessities, may seem insignificant on a grander scale, but the intent of *The Samaritan
Project* is offering tangible help to those who feel they are
sinking. With great love, we became a community of active
lids for one another.

Time has delivered to me the unshakable truth that we
are never alone. Even in the darkest hour, there is that unde-
niable presence of a greater power that waits patiently for
its recognition —that power is God. When my relationship
with God continues to shift from the adolescent fear of a
white-bearded judgmental old man in the sky to an omni-
present companion whose love for me defies words, then
my heart relaxes, my fears dissolve, and I embrace Spirit
with an intimacy not found in human contact. I write:

> *You are my star,*
> *my divining rod that*
> *leads me to oceans*
> *of comfort and*
> *childlike curiosity*
> *where I laugh*
> *during the exploration*
> *and dance in my dreams.*
> *You are my carved arrow*
> *nailed to the oak,*
> *tireless in your pointing*

to the path that leads
to our union.
I rip at the vines and
candle the dark to see you there
smiling.
And I am your reflection
joined forever.

God is everywhere present. In and through all things—the most reliable lid that ever was. That Spirit lives as boat operator, big sister, cheerleader, ancient heartbeat, bird song, and friend. We are asked to be nothing less.

When the master teacher Jesus spoke to his disciples saying, "I will make you fishers of men," his charge was to go and lift people's spirits from drowning in illusion. Likewise, when we act as lids, we become compassionate lifelines helping humanity come up for air.

Joseph Campbell wrote, "When we quit thinking primarily about ourselves and our own self-preservation, we undergo a truly heroic transformation of consciousness." My awareness agrees, yet I realize the paradoxical importance of extending that helping hand to myself. We must also become our own lids. Our love of self must be such that we give ourselves the same compassionate gifts of understanding, patience, and care that we would give to anyone else.

Months later, I returned to the Huntington Gardens. The temperature is warmer, and the grass seems somewhat faded by the persistent summer sun. Even the spring blooms have disappeared and given way to a new crop of showy foliage. But, with closer inspection, the lids of border grass still thrive, constant in their job to showcase and house their seasonal friends. I pray to be just like them.

1) Who were the most significant lids of your past?

2) Who are the most significant lids in your life now?

3) Are there any individuals who have made both lists? If so, what are the qualities of support they have demonstrated? Are you willing to offer those qualities to yourself?

The Parable Of The Tea Kettle

Living in Southern California, it is safe to say we are one of Mother Nature's favorite children. So, when inclement weather occurs, we rush into the nearest drug store purchasing our umpteenth umbrella. Somewhere at home or in the trunk of the car is a forgotten graveyard of these things. Do we even remember how to use them? We may never forget how to ride a bike, but we are a subculture that just might benefit from repeated instructions on how to operate that invention of moisture protection.

The advent of rain tends to produce paralyzing crankiness. When El Niño descended upon us with its torrential downpours there were days when the city often came to a virtual standstill. In the beginning of 1999, it seemed as though it rained all of January, February and March.

Synchronized with the enduring showers was the por-

25

tentous winter flu season that infiltrated its way into the psyches of mass consciousness through advertisements for cough syrups, liquid night time reliefs and evening news programs proclaiming, it's here! If the rain didn't wreak havoc on our lives then, by golly, the flu bug would.

Like most everyone I knew, I invited the bug into my home.

I seemed to have rolled out some unconscious welcome mat while my southern upbringing yelled out "howdy" and "mi casa es su casa."

I ate with it. I slept with it. I watched bad television with it. It made its presence known and I finally stopped trying to resist its visit. We "vacationed" this way for about a week, and I was comfortable in letting the bug see me in all my flu-like glory with greasy bed-head, beard growth and dishes piled like Pisa's landmark in my sink.

After about a week, its visitation time drew to a close.

Maybe it was getting restless. Maybe it had some other unsuspecting office worker, schoolteacher, or grocery clerk in the area that it missed. Maybe there was a quota to fill during its season like the highway patrol on the Pasadena freeway. In any event, I felt dramatically better and after changing the sheets, and a homecoming with the shower, I felt human again.

Jumping back into work, I plodded through an avalanche of e-mail, phone calls and bookings, tiring after only a few hours. After one day, I was back in bed with a surprise return visit from my unrelenting house guest.

And thus began the cycle of the flu returning and leaving, returning and leaving, spawning a "tete-a-tete" that contained all the trappings of a really dysfunctional relationship.

So, between the plentiful rain and plentiful flu, I was not in a plentiful state of peace.

Searching for clues through the rubble of my present circumstances, no answer seemed primed for excavation. No explanation surfaced for this unseemly courtship. Yet, taking on the eyes of a tailor, I examined the situation more closely and decided some lifestyle choices needed altering.

I like my coffee in the morning like most people, but after noon, I'm pretty much done with hot beverages. The teakettle, however, became my all-day, all-night support friend. I was not accustomed to drinking tea but daily brews of echinacea and honey and lemon concoctions were fast becoming routine. The howling steam from the kettle seemed to cry out like a territorial wolf, daring that flu to enter its space. Ignore the warning and there was sure to be the fight that legends are made of.

Daily tea making was now in full swing.

There were the loose-leaf variations that required the fancy strainer yet, I leaned toward the prepackaged varieties that promised everything from coating my throat to freeing my lungs.

"I could use a little lung freeing," I thought.

Days of faithful tea sipping occurred and I was on the mend.

Not only was I feeling like my old self again, but so was Southern California.

27

The once familiar sun was making its way back into our daily lives, and we secretly vowed that if it did, we would never take its presence for granted again.

It was time to celebrate, and I placed the full kettle on the burner to create my brew for the day. Waiting for the water to boil, I felt rather "wild" and "dangerous." Mixing echinacea with things like licorice root, fenugreek and meadowsweet, I was tea man riding full throttle on my herb motorcycle.

I opened my front door and stepped out onto the porch.

Lying there, where I'd left them weeks before, were my pair of orange-handled pruning shears. Taking in the view, I could see the yard looked rather neglected since the deluge, so I grabbed the shears and went off on a peripheral clip job.

I am an avid gardener. I love it. You give me a hoe, a spade, a rake or pruning shears and I lose all track of time. I love my hands in the earth, the way I feel when I'm connected to the soil. Sometimes I'm surprised to find an entire day has gone by, and I am still weeding and digging away.

On this particular occasion, thankfully, my reverie only lasted about an hour and a half. Yet, it was just long enough that when I stepped back into the house, a really awful burning stench emanated from the kitchen.

"The teakettle!" I yelled and off I raced toward the stove. I turned the burner off, grabbed the kitchen mitt and set the kettle in the sink.

Not only was it completely charred and blackened all the way around, but it had also caved in on both sides as if some appliance corset had sadistically and cruelly cinched it in.

That old American Tourister luggage commercial came to mind. The unsuspecting luggage was tossed into a cage with a gorilla who took it and banged it mercilessly against the bars and floor. Miraculously, it survived unscathed and unscratched. My teakettle seemed to have "gone into the cage" yet hadn't faired as well.

My little metal friend had passed into appliance heaven thanks to my neglect.

On my way to purchase a new teakettle, I wondered what advanced technologies might have been invented for them and if there were some brands that came with built in sirens or buzzers for careless owners.

Genuinely thankful that nothing more serious had happened, I became amused at the insightful metaphor that had played out before my eyes.

I realized that I am the teakettle. God is the flame.

I am filled with this fluidity, these passions and desires. God is igniting all of this within me, encouraging its movement and beckoning me to do something with the ideas that live in my heart.

Long ago, I began to understand that the desires of the heart are not placed there to torture us. God could never do that, for God is and always has been love. To dangle the proverbial carrot to get us to be subservient or obedient does not even register within the Divine.

My passion for music is not given to me to ignore even though I may have been taught I can't make a respectable

29

living singing. An interest in sculpting didn't just surface for someone else to become frustrated working at a more sensible and safe profession. Something is drawing each one of us to examine more fully what role that creative urge is begging to play in our lives. It is the call. It is constant.

Like the teakettle, that call is forever sounding off, whistling, shouting its presence to us to notice and pick it up. And yet, so often we don't.

We go off somewhere to prune a non-threatening bush, toil with some insignificant weeds, and turn a deaf ear. We create any number of distractions to avoid the call, preventing us, most notably from saying yes!

We divert our attentions to someone else's problem or situation. At times, we expend more energy in avoiding the call than if we surrendered, saying, "OK, I'll do it. I don't know how it will happen or how it will unfold but I'm willing to take that first step."

Once that decision is made, the Universe knows a way to match us where we are and bring our desires to demonstration.

Saying yes to that divine urging could mean we might have to set aside, once and for all, thoughts of not being good enough or smart enough. Or, it could mean that we are willing, at least, to shed new light on the consideration that our worries are unfounded. That could certainly create a backlash from old stagnant ideas! That familiar committee might naggingly whisper to us that there are dozens of others who will do it much better than we can, so why bother?

Is it any wonder, then, after decades of avoiding this

call, we feel so burned by life, charred by experiences and disposable?

I envision if we did say yes, the Universe would act like a supportive arm coming down and picking up the whistling teakettle, pouring us into an experience that not only nourishes us but also nourishes the world.

So, why are we so afraid? Why have so many of us chosen to neglect our passions for a less than second-best existence?

The years I traveled and performed as a member of the vocal trio Alliance with metaphysician and lecturer Louise Hay were eye opening. It did not matter what part of the country we were in, what economic bracket of the people we were performing for, or what current issue or circumstance it was that they were going through. Everyone struggled with accepting his or her own personal divinity. Without exception, I observed the difficulty people had in loving the self or even resting in the possibility that where they were in that moment of awareness or experience was enough. What would it take to give ourselves the same degree of acceptance that we seem so readily willing to give to others? We are experts in self-flogging.

I recalled the story of a little Catholic girl who began to have visitations from the master teacher Jesus. As any child might, she felt a state of wonderment and awe at being singled out with these loving conversations and wanted desperately to share her experiences with someone.

The enthusiastic girl went to her priest and told him the miraculous news.

31

"Jesus comes and talks with me, and we have such a wonderful time," she said, her eyes glowing with excitement.

The priest listened but did not take the child seriously. After all, wouldn't a miracle such as this happen with someone who was more spiritually mature and able to pass on the information to the masses?

Someone like himself?

Yet, day after day she came to the priest and recounted her visitations. They were simple but joyous stories in which Jesus said that she was loved, and she must never forget that.

The priest continued to listen but soon grew agitated with the girl. By repeatedly listening, he felt he was encouraging her to continue telling "tall tales."

He labored over ways to end this charade once and for all. At last he had a plan.

"Another visit?" he asked rather sarcastically upon seeing his young guest.

"Oh, yes," she said and began to tell him of their latest exchange.

The priest stopped her before she could finish.

"Will you do me a favor?" he asked.

"Of course," said the girl.

"The next time Jesus comes for a visit, will you ask him a question for me?"

"Yes," she agreed.

"Will you ask him what it was that I did that was so terrible when I was studying to be a priest?"

The little girl's eyes conveyed her confusion.

"I want you to ask Jesus what it was that I did that was so terrible when I was studying to be a priest," he emphatically repeated. "Will you do that?"

She responded that she would and left his office.

He felt confident that he had put an end to her over imaginative stories.

When a few days went by and the little girl had not visited him, he grew even more proud of his clever plan. The priest knew that the little girl could not come back and reveal another visit without divulging his darkest secret. That would never happen. He had never told a soul.

Weeks later, while crossing the parish grounds, he chanced upon her playing with some of the other children.

"Hello," he said to her. "You haven't been back to see me."

"My mother's been quite ill, and my father needed me to stay home and help care for her so he could continue working."

"I suppose, then, the visitations have stopped?" inquired the priest.

"Oh no," she said. "In fact, he came and sat with my mother and me for the longest time."

Upon hearing this, the priest began to get a bit nervous.

"Do you remember our agreement?" he questioned quietly.

"Yes," she answered calmly.

Swallowing hard, the priest wiped the sweat from his forehead and questioned, "You asked Jesus what it was that

33

I did that was so terrible when I was studying to be a priest?"

"Yes," she again replied.

"My God, child, what did he say?" pulling her off to the side.

"He told me to tell you, he doesn't remember."

This story has been a favorite for years for it beautifully illustrates how we are the best score card keepers of our past mistakes. We mentally check off how many times we have fallen and failed, thinking that the rest of the world must be keeping the same tally of shame.

No one could be more punishing or a harsher critic.

I did some serious examining of my own personal history with self-love and this dance of desire.

I've sat more times than I care to admit in the chair of indecision and fear, fidgeting in my seat of lack and limitation while my life's purpose waltzed solo on the dance floor of boundless possibility.

Sitting there doesn't make the calling stop. It just keeps dancing inside us. The teakettle just keeps whistling. We either get better at becoming blind and deaf to it, or we give in and start the journey toward the fulfillment of being what it is we came here to be.

1) List 5 passions/divine urgings that still dwell within and beckon you to explore taking an action.

2) What commentary does your "inner critic" provide when you consider investigating these passions?

3) Instead of a score card focused on every failure or mistake, or you willing to devote your energy in creating a new score card—one that lists your triumphs, great or small, subtle or publicly acknowledged? What you focus your energy on, you empower and bring into form. Which score card is going to serve your divine purpose?

Ducks In A Row

The mother duck gave birth to four little feathered dar-
lings. Though her love for them was genuine, she could not
seem to stop the ripple of worry that kept on growing and
growing.

"How will my young ones fair in such an unpredictable world?" she questioned. After all, her life had been one
upstream struggle after the next, what with contaminated
ponds, poachers and good for nothing mallards who had
left her with shallow promises and a broken heart. But now,
as a new mother, her soul seemed to fluctuate with paradoxical elation and paralyzing fear over this new milestone
in her life.

It was a messy, lonely birth.

When duckling number one started to hatch through
the speckled shell, the mother could not stop thinking about

37

the mallard that had abandoned her at this sensitive time.

"Relationships are painful and tough," she sighed as the first tiny duckling squeaked and squirmed. In keeping with her present thoughts, she gave this newborn the unlikely name Relationship.

Pondering her future, the mother duck envisioned how everything would be changing.

She'd always fancied a career as the head flyer in one of those V-formations, but now, with a family to raise, that dream would be put on hold indefinitely. She couldn't be flying off to points South whenever she felt like it. Responsibilities were now curbing her ambitions. Soon duckling number two broke through its egg home and because of her current daydreaming, the mother named this one Career.

Being a single duck with new mouths to feed opened up a whole new can of worms.

"Actually," she quacked at the thought, "worms mixed with a little gruel would be a real treat right now. Whoever believed the can of worms expression to be negative obviously didn't have little beaks to fill."

The mother's thoughts stormed with concern about providing for her new burgeoning family, for her financial duckfolio was sketchy at best. She regretted having fouled up in the savings department. And, as this emotional whirlwind was reaching its anxious peak, duckling number three arrived. Because of her current contemplation, she decided to name this newest addition Finances.

Her once dormant mothering instincts now actively revealed she was not quite finished.

"Deliver me from mint jelly," she snapped in frustration, "but this birthing business really takes it out of you!"

Having once paddled after wellness with a vengeance, she now lingered on the implausible task of regaining her fine-feathered figure.

Before, vibrant health was effortless for her, contributing to her numerous title holdings as Miss Beat The Skeet. But, the ramifications of having a family would undoubtedly change all of that. Hadn't her own mother succumbed to the kind of waddle that made others snicker through their beaks? The painful memories washed over her with the dread of her supposed fate.

At that precise moment, with a tiny, lyrical peep the fourth and final duckling announced its arrival. In keeping with the rest of the naming process, she christened this last little one, Health.

And now Relationship, Career, Finances and Health swam behind their mother, developing and growing instinctively in their vast watery playground.

The pond was a hubbub of varied characters that interacted with mother and the duckling four on their daily routine.

There were, of course, the other ducks offering unsolicited advice on how the newborns should be raised. The old guard believed in spare the beak bite, spoil the duckling while others swore the benefits of a regimented algae diet.

"Feed them that and you'll never have to worry about Attention Duckling Deficit Disorder!"

"Whatever you do, keep 'em quiet!" demanded the tree

perching crows, "lest they scare away our potential meals."

The disgruntled frog community complained of the excess ripples, their lily pads wobbling to and fro from the motion.

"Whoa with the paddling," they croaked! "You're scaring the flies!"

Even the crickets in the reeded grass and the air born dragonflies seemed to chirp their interpretation of the territorial rules.

The mother felt she was already being plucked from all sides without the interference from the populace, but she secretly listened in case some useful parental formula was cast out with the rest of the drivel.

She heard none.

Instead, everyone seemed to voice how difficult it was to raise a family and, like it or not, life would always be about the survival of the fittest.

Sacrifice, compromise, disorder and chaos were the lyrics in this diverse collective's woeful chant.

The mother began feeling a terrible sense of uneasiness in the pit of her stomach.

"If they've already been through this, then they must know. They must be telling the truth."

Weighted down by an ever-growing depression, she recalled her own formative years and remembered the stoic determination of her own mother. She'd watched her become thick-skinned but inwardly defeated.

"I picked this pond. I'll just have to swim in it," she remembered her saying.

Thus life, at this point, became about making do.

Little Relationship was very outgoing and approached everyone with naive zeal.

"Hey there, my name's Relationship and next week my mother says I'll have grown into my flying wings! Do you have flying wings?" The other ducks halfheartedly listened, their jaded attitudes stealing their ability to even look at the little one.

"Go away. We're busy!"

Undaunted, Relationship kept announcing his upcoming adventure.

"Do you have flying wings?"

The frogs became annoyed and accused him of making fun of them.

"You know we can't fly. Why would you ask such a stupid question?" And with that the frogs unleashed their tongues and snapped at his feathers.

"Relationship! Get back here! The mother cried. "Don't ever swim out of line unless I say you can!"

Relationship became sad, for more than anything he wanted to make friends and communicate. What he experienced was disinterest or misunderstandings.

Little Career seemed fixated by the sky. Every time a bird flew over head her heart beat faster and a rush of adrenaline made her wish she were flying beside them. She would stretch at her under-developed wings and long for the day when she could share in their boundless view.

One day, a bird far mightier in stature and grander than any other floated silently above Career.

41

She stared in awe.

"Who is that, Mother?" she questioned unable to take her eyes off its grace and agility.

"That's an eagle, dear one," she answered. Her tone taking on a hushed reverence.

"They are the rulers of our skies, the mightiest of us all."

"Then I want to be an eagle when I grow up," enthused Career.

"Hush," said mother, hoping that the great one had not heard.

"You are a duck. You can never be an eagle. You can never explore the skies like them for your life is destined for migration. Period. The sooner you get used to that, the easier your life will be.

And besides, you'll have ducklings of your own some day. It wouldn't be very proper for a girl to go exploring the skies when her role is to stay at home, now would it? You'll learn to do just as I am doing, raising a family."

The mother felt a twinge of regret run through her. She knew in that unretractable moment that she dampened the dream of her little one just as her own mother had dampened hers.

"It's for the best," she reasoned but could not bear to look into Career's crestfallen eyes.

As the days passed, so did the maturity of the ducklings. Each worked at becoming adept at the flying exercises their mother put them through. From fence railings to low lying tree branches, the ducklings advanced higher with the growing strength of their wings.

Finances showed impressive strength and often cheered his other siblings. He seemed to have an innate desire for everyone to win and was generous with his encouragement.

Resting comfortably on a tree branch after a practice run, Finances' gaze settled on the adjacent meadow down below. It was a dizzying display of activity that rivaled his own pond. Gray squirrel hopped frenetically among the littered acorns, and rabbit seemed exceptionally content as she feasted on thick grass and lettuce.

"Lettuce!" young Finances exclaimed. "Where did she get lettuce?"

With fixated eyes, he followed several other zigzag hopping rabbits. As they rounded a bush, Finances flew toward another tree to keep them in view—then another and another, until the rabbits came to rest in a garden some distance away. There, in neat succession, were rows and rows of the green stuff.

Without hesitation, Finances flapped and flew over to the garden, landing with the grace of a duck that had been flying forever. In his excitement, he had totally forgotten about the distance, as his instincts seemed to kick in naturally.

Before him lay an inexhaustible treasure—a never-ending banquet of leafy greens.

"There is enough to feed everyone at home until winter calls," calculated Finances.

Though some wouldn't appreciate a steady diet of lettuce, others, such as the frogs, could feast on the bugs that lived contentedly between the leaves.

43

Finances flew back to tell Mother the great news.

She scolded him for leaving her sight, but paused long enough when the field of lettuce was mentioned.

"A whole garden of lettuce?" repeated Mother. "Show me."

With all four tucked around her feet, the mother stressed that no one, under any circumstances, should talk of the garden.

"We must keep this a secret," she whispered. "If we let everyone else know, then we'll all be fighting over ownership."

"But, mother, there's plenty for everyone," said Finances. "Why can't we all share?"

"You're too young to understand," she hastened, "but believe you me, there are those who would clear this all out before you could say perfect plumage! No, we need to take care of ourselves. Promise me you will not tell a soul about this."

Each one promised, yet Finances felt the beginnings of an unexplainable anxiety inside him. If the rest of the pond's inhabitants were that thoughtless and stingy, then one should only fend for oneself—one could never know when there might not be enough.

As Relationship, Career and Finances continued growing in strength and stamina, little Health struggled to keep up. She heard the word puny whispered when the others in the duck community spoke of her. Health's coloring was not as brilliant as her brothers or richly refined as her sisters. Some were generous in their comparisons to the well-known ugly duckling story. And, placing wagers on whether anything of beauty could evolve from her current countenance, the consensus among the pond dwellers believed it unlikely.

Was it disappointment she imagined in her mother's eyes or simply concern?

She couldn't decide which was worse because even the latter meant that she was somehow a burden.

Health decided that no matter what, she would push herself to be as productive as the others and free her mother of any worry.

When her three siblings attempted the latest flying maneuver, Health tagged right along, straining her spindly wingspan and gasping for air. She struggled with the landing and on several occasions missed the branch entirely. She felt the stinging cold penetrate her underdeveloped body when pond-dipping for bugs. The water's temperature contributed to uncontrollable shivering, forcing her mother to come and blanket her with her wing. Health knew that this broke the all-important daily routine and was embarrassed she required the attention.

"Why can't I just be like everyone else?" she sighed in disgust.

No matter how hard she compensated, Health's weak constitution was always creating a mishap or delay. Her breathing became increasingly labored until one morning, she was unable to move from the nest.

The mother panicked and started collecting small bugs and algae to help feed her daughter.

45

"Come on Health, you've got to eat this to regain your strength!

Little Health could only lie there and obey, not even having the energy to be embarrassed.

Relationship, Career and Finances gave up their flying lessons to help with the food collecting, but it seemed to be touch and go for quite some time.

The mother's anguish was unbearable, watching her young duckling struggle for life. She coddled and cooed at her. She altered her rigid, traditional views and whispered that if little Health got better, she could grow up to be anything she dreamed of. The prayerful watch continued.

Health began to realize that her mother must really love her to be expending such efforts in her recovery. Her affections were not based on Health's productivity. Mother loved her because of who she was not because of what was expected of her.

The attention and care was paying off, and Health was able to sit up and stretch her wings. Something felt different in her. It was as if this familial bonding had healed the thoughts of inadequacy that had weakened her body and spirit. There was no longer a sense of foreboding—a belief that she would never be able to keep up.

She simply felt loved and cared for, creating the best medicine of all.

There was a shift in her mother as well.

Her approach to raising the four ducklings softened and she gave them liberties to explore and discover what their pond world held for them. If the expression "I can't"

46

ever rang out from the young ones, Mother immediately told them the alternative. Every day, she encouraged them to believe in themselves, to let go of their fears and limitations.

Adopting her own advice, Mother let go of old ideas that were weighing her down.

She no longer focused her attention on the difficulty of raising a family but felt blessed by the opportunity. The outpouring of love towards her little ones had rippled its magic back to her.

"It is possible to have all my ducks in a row," she discovered.

Most of us struggle with beliefs like the mother did in the beginning of the story. It is hard for us to fathom that we can have simultaneous bliss in the four categories of Relationship, Career, Finances and Health. There is an undercurrent in our belief system that suggests one or another of these areas must suffer in order for the remaining to have their time in the sun. We struggle with the idea of having our "ducks in a row." If one duck is riding the crest of the wave, one or all of the others must be drowning, plucked or shot at.

How many times have we allowed intimacy into our lives only to have our career suffer or get our finances in order only to have a health challenge escort us back into debt? Career blossoms only to have health issues dampen our prospects—finances are flourishing only to have our marriage disintegrate, etc.

I have observed this phenomenon in so many that I had

47

to look at my personal participation in it.

I, too, believed that it was virtually impossible to have all the "ducks swimming blissfully in a row."

I uncovered an old belief that dictated that one or more must be sacrificed in order for the others to be successful.

Pinpointing the exact moment that belief was adopted can be traced back to 1967.

My father, Pete, suffered from heart disease a great deal of his adult life.

Frequently, in and out of the Veteran's Hospital in Houston, interacting with him can only be found in the slightest memories. In March of 1967, he finally relinquished his struggle and died from heart failure at the ripe old age of 54.

I was seven years old, the last of five children and part of a household that scrimped for the meager means to survive. Dad's death only exacerbated the situation.

Our home was a flat-topped abode in great need of repair, and with four out of the five children still under one roof, there simply weren't enough bedrooms to go around. I was relegated to a cot-bed in the corner of my parent's bedroom.

When the phone rang in that pre-dawn hour, I listened in the darkness as my mother spoke with a hospital administrator. She took down the information and kept responding with either a yes or I see. As the conversation ended, she paused for a moment and then began phoning my aunt.

The sound of the rotary dial clicked in rhythm with the choir of crickets hastening to get in their last musical efforts before sunrise. Intuitively knowing this was serious, I sat up, leaned against the wall behind my bed and wrapped my arms around my pillow. Its pliable form became my home made shield.

After apologizing for the hour, my mother told her that my father had died of a heart attack.

Then, with frustration in her voice said, "Now what am I supposed to do with a seven year old boy?"

The pillow didn't work. The words pierced my heart.

Hearing these words, my seven-year-old interpretation was that somehow this was my fault.

Children's minds work in fascinating and inexplicable ways.

My mother never actually said it was my fault, but I determined from the comment that I was a burden, that I was going to have to work very hard in order to be worthy enough to remain in that household. Then and there, I took responsibility for my father's death.

When the actual memory of this resurfaced in my adult years, I recognized how beautifully this adopted belief system had played itself out in my life. I was a champion super achiever—not because I always liked every task, but because I thought it would please my mother, friends, teachers or love interest. In order to be accepted, I must do before asked, taking responsibility for everyone's happiness before my own. This demon of unworthiness was like an unquenchable thirst, yet all I seemed to do was fill everyone else's glass.

Popular author Carolyn Myss once presented an idea called the Six Second Theory. She stated that something that literally could have taken six seconds still governs what we think about ourselves to this very day. Six seconds! That's not a long time and yet in that fraction of a minute, careless words can leave lasting impressions.

You may have had a second grade teacher say something like, "I just want you to mouth the words. OK?" Even with a great love for singing, that 6 seconds helped bury that love and formulate a decision to stop altogether. It could have been an off-hand comment from a parent or sibling, but it chiseled away at your core foundation creating a belief about yourself that was thought of as truth.

Those comments were molds into which we poured ourselves, letting an identity take form that would rule our entire lives.

Nothing could be further from the truth.

When I realized the power and validity I had given my mother's comment, I had one of those sky opening, angel singing, a-ha moments.

What my mother said really had nothing to do with me. It was simply the frustrated expression of a woman who was sad, frightened about the future and worried about feeding all of us. It had nothing to do with me personally. Yet, the internalized lie made it feel like it had everything to do with me.

Whatever six second moment you are holding on to, the one that gets in your way and holds you back from your greatness, well, it has nothing to do with you either.

Those seconds might be the opinions or fears of people who are dealing with their own survival, with their own collective six seconds. As we recognize this, we can begin to disrupt the contagion of despair, anxiety and hopelessness that we mindlessly pass on to one another.

Our unbelief in a "ducks in a row" existence comes from someone else's opinion—it is often colored from their own history of fear and disappointment and thus, we let it color ours. Most likely, the erroneous beliefs have passed from parent or elder creating a diseased family tree. They serve no purpose for our present experience.

I was told that life was hard, challenging and sacrificial. Everything I observed supported that. There was little that floated in the air of that Southeast Texas home that encouraged a belief other than basic survival saturated with worry.

But, the possibility of transformation can root in the most malnourished soil. The indestructible seed is the willingness to change our belief.

Remembering the words of Matthew 21, we are instructed that whatever we ask for in prayer, believing, we will receive. This scripture is a simple reminder that God gives us the desires of our heart if we believe in our worthiness to receive them. This principle's manifestation isn't based on our past as saint or transgressor. It is a law, activated by our current state of consciousness. Likewise, Luke 12 teaches that it is God's great pleasure to give us the kingdom. Not just an alleyway or a portion deemed suitably matched to our life's accomplishments, but the kingdom — the kingdom, the whole kingdom and nothing but the kingdom so help God's pleasure. We must retrain our minds to

51

embrace this belief.

To illustrate this point, when we place an order in a restaurant, we believe that what we ordered will be served us. Seldom do we find ourselves worrying and doubting that our request will be met. We don't follow the waiter back to the kitchen and stand in front of the chef to make sure that the specifications are met. We simply place the order and expect it to be delivered. We believe in the process.

We believe that everyone will follow the rules of driving every time we start the car and venture on the streets and freeways.

If we believe in these things, simple and common, can't we believe that our prayers are answered? Can't we believe that God will provide in all areas at all times?

By allowing our prayers to be cast in waters of absolute faith, then every facet of our life thrives in equanimity—our ducks swim harmoniously in sweet demonstration.

1) *Of the four qualities listed in this story, Relationship, Career, Finances and Health, which ones in your life are flourishing and which ones are not.*

2) *What is your belief that all of these can work optimally in your life at the same time.*

3) *Is there a 6 second moment that you are holding onto that is getting in the way of having all your ducks in a row?*

The Old Beloved

I persistently ignored an inner calling involving an ancient civilization, a sacred site and a haunting. The civilization was Incan, the site Machu Picchu in Peru, the haunting, the diligent Andean images that followed me like a twenty-four hour shadow.

As far back as 1981, a South American travel book enticed this wanderlust window shopper. Something jumped out of the four-color, glossy photos of the famous ruins with the zeal of a cricket escaping my long ago juvenile grasp. My breath stalled. Standing on a sidewalk in New York City, I peered through the display window of my neighborhood bookstore. Skyward pools of delicate mist, lush green foliage and massive stone formations stuck to my soul like flypaper on a southern porch. Everything internally beckoned me not to break my gaze. Pressing my face to the glass,

55

I seemed to forget that I could simply walk in and look at the book on display. Reason seemed lost, however, because I could not take my eyes off this source of intoxication.

I knew that I was supposed to go there. I knew it as clearly as my name.

What finally broke the trance has long been forgotten, but I recalled walking away saying, "I've got to buy that book someday."

Everything was someday back then.

As an actor paying New York rent and personifying all aspects of the struggling artist's syndrome, I shifted nearly every desire outside the realm of basic survival to the future. Words like impractical, impossible, implausible—all those "im" words constantly followed the other use of those two letters—I'm.

My mind didn't even register the possibility of actually going to Peru. I just wanted the book. Now that I knew of Machu Picchu's existence, a barrage of photos of this Andean fortress teased me with great regularity. Old issues of National Geographic or the travel section of The New York Times would periodically highlight this ancient wonder and I'd dutifully clip and save them. I soon felt absorbed in all things Incan.

Shirley MacLaine later followed with her popular *Out On a Limb* adventures and I began to think, true to form, "Maybe I'll get there someday."

Years following that first sighting passed as if under the command of an unpredictable remote control device. At times the finger of the universe seemed to be pressing fast forward. At other times, it stopped each daily frame with immovable scrutiny while the adventures of life played out their paradoxical spectrum. Human drama showed its range by performing the high art of Shakespeare to embarrassing episodes of *Days of Our Lives*.

My acting was dually represented. As a human being I seemed to be living the latter.

It was time for a change.

The century old echo, "go west young man," wafted its way through the streets of Manhattan and whispered mercilessly in my ears. It just didn't come with an instruction manual. My friend, Hope, and I joked that we would refrain from the coast-to-coast show business migration, proudly displaying an eventual tombstone that would read "Succeeded In Show Business without Living in Los Angeles."

"Be strong," she'd encourage, all the while horrified as the reflection of palm trees grew in my pupils.

Eventually the palm trees won, and I found myself doing something I swore I'd never do, writing my first rent check in Los Angeles. Funny those things we swear we won't do. It's as if, once we declare the swear, the feasibility of the event actually taking place comes rushing in with forcible swiftness and strength. Los Angeles was a great magnetic creature and I, a lightweight paperclip whose resistance was futile.

Strolling down Melrose Avenue one day, I attempted to coordinate my meandering while eating a messy Mediterranean sandwich with an unpronounceable name. It dripped all over my hands and face and I postured like Quasimodo to keep it off my shirt. Hunched over, I wasn't paying attention and nearly knocked over a guy exiting a storefront.

Jerry Florence, a friend from my college days, stood before me, moist from a mixture of cucumber and humus.

"So this is how you say hello?" he joked as I wiped my hands and memory clear of the cobwebs from all the years since I'd seen him.

It is a reunion that changed the course of my life.

Jerry introduced me to metaphysics, authors Louise Hay, and Marianne Williamson and *A Course in Miracles*. Through these paths, I discovered the philosophies of Religious Science and Unity and began to realize that the belief system of my childhood no longer served me. With Jerry and his partner Keith Kimberlin, we began our journey as the musical trio, Alliance. A new form of music found its birth and we began singing at inspirational venues all over the country. Notoriety grew. So did the epidemic of AIDS, and we watched its unrelenting descent upon our lives. Performing with notable authors and speakers from Louise Hay to Gerry Jampolsky to Dr. Carl Simonton we were intent on bringing some sanity and hope to an insane situation. Sitting bedside for countless good-byes to friends became a numbing ritual—Jerry and Keith's among them.

Adulthood and responsibility were spilling out on life's counter top and I felt like a dutiful sponge.

"Buck up David. Be a man," the inner voice would taunt. Truthfully, all I wanted to do was shut the door to the world and cry.

Yet, I had become too involved in this work to casually

walk away. Some small inner voice reminiscent of the one in the movie *Field of Dreams* kept prompting, "Go the distance." But where? Apprehensive to approach a musical career on my own, the thought of soloing felt lonely and strangely inappropriate. Jerry and Keith had been my stage buddies. When one of us felt out of sorts, the other two would carry the weight. Now, alone, I ached for my friends, feeling foolish at my naïve assumptions that they would always be there.

Despite the grief, the "go the distance" seed had been planted and that mantra repeatedly harvested itself. Responsibility to carry the torch meshed with the duty to answer the call. Self-doubt was pushed aside. Logging thousands of miles with thousands of life lessons, I settled into this new creative format over the ensuing years. And, before the birthday fairy could taunt, "Where'd your life go?" I was preparing to greet the big four—oh.

Could I have actually been alive and functioning on this planet for forty years?

Truthfully, I was grateful to get this far. It was sobering to think of so many friends who never made this milestone and I began to think more deeply about what I wanted to do as the second half of my life approached.

Never far away were my thoughts of Peru.

Driving in my car, one day in spring, my eyes flashed on the license plate in front of me. It spelled out PERU. I entertained a myriad of scenarios about how the driver got from the Andes to Los Angeles when I looked up to see a small billboard that simply read "Why Not?"

59

First PERU, then Why Not?

License plate—billboard. License plate—billboard.

Peru—why not? Peru—why not?

I stopped at a grocery store to pick up a few things and turned to go down the cereal aisle.

Nothing unusual. Yet, this day, the boxes all seemed to be arranged in such a way as to spell out those same four letters.

P - E - R - U. Trying to rub the image from my eyes, the multi-grain display steadfastly continued its spelling lesson. Was this Peru awareness week and I had not been notified?

At home, I propped myself on the back patio with a bowl of cereal in one hand and the Los Angeles Sunday Times in the other. The travel section featured a writer's recent adventure on the Inca Trail. His story marveled on the adventure of hiking this famous path, which opens onto the ruins of Machu Picchu. There, in four-color splendor, was the same breathtaking image that launched this desire so many years before.

"OK, enough." I thought. It's now or never."

I knew that upon my June birthday arrival I would qualify to start checking off a different age bracket on insurance surveys and the occasional audition form that one filled out in waiting rooms all over Hollywood.

What better way to celebrate this milestone than in Peru? Suddenly the idea was no longer far-fetched. Ceremoniously, I cancelled my itinerary for the entire month of June. I was going.

"Just get there," my inner voice said, "Everything else will be handled."

The ticket price, quoted from a small agency in Koreatown, was amazingly reasonable.

"This is a cash-only transaction," the agent said. I wondered what other "businesses" might be lurking behind the wall of travel posters. Nonetheless, the airlines confirmed I possessed a legitimate round-trip ticket from Los Angeles to Lima. In an unprecedented style of behavior, I decided to make no reservations in between my South American arrival and my California return. The precisioned planner inside me was going to have to take a rest. Something patiently called me towards this journey for half my life and I was going to show up, without agenda, and follow attentively.

My friend, Maureen, planned a huge birthday celebration. Surprisingly, she suggested that if they felt so moved, the attendees could consider making contributions towards my trip. Between chants of "lordy, lordy look who's forty" I felt loved and supported. Suddenly this bare-bones trip was not going to have to be so bare-boned.

I arrived in Lima. Instinctively I knew that this was not some place I wished to stay. The eight million people inhabiting this city faced incredible pollution. The air was thick with emissions from thousands of unregulated diesel-burning cars and buses. The taxi that drove me to the section known as Miraflores turned its lights on in the middle of the day. The open window sent warm blasts of air that stung

61

my eyes and burned the walls of my lungs.

"Not the most spectacular beginning," I thought, but I knew where I really wanted to go.

I found a hotel for the night and set about making plans to get to the city of Cusco.

Cusco means navel. It was the historic center of the Incan Empire. This "small" city of three hundred thousand people was legendary for having been the epicenter for what was once one of the most powerful civilizations in the world. The ruling empire stretched far past the borders of Peru into what we know today as Chile and Bolivia. Like the initial draw that came from seeing that first photo of Machu Picchu, Cusco seemed to whisper, "get here." Less than 24 hours later I dutifully obeyed. Any guidebook will forewarn visitors that you are about to make a major altitude adjustment. The city is 14,000 feet above sea level and I was cautioned to take it slow and easy. Caution seemed an inappropriate mix with my enveloping excitement.

I grabbed my backpack and duffel and stepped out into the thin air and spectacular blue sky.

When my foot hit the tarmac I was overcome by a surprising wave of emotion. Like grateful soldiers returning to their homeland after time away in battle, I began to cry and impulsively thought of dropping to my knees and kissing the ground.

What was this all about?

The more I tried to suppress or control the tears, the more they persisted.

"Get a grip David!" I charged. "All these people are

looking at you!"

Suddenly, I realized, "I'm in South America for God's sake! No one knows who I am. Cry away!"

And cry I did. Not soft little controllable discharges, mind you. These were sobs of incredible emotion.

In hindsight, I must have looked somewhat freakish, backpack and duffel in tow as I maneuvered my way into town still crying. The locals shifted their strides to the other side of the street. My tears were not about anything remotely related to grief or sorrow. These were tears of joy.

"Such joy does exist." I discovered.

"There was that blue sky again," I noticed through watery eyes, its hue reminiscent of a child's crayon on pristine paper, colored with purity and freedom.

Within the hour, I discovered the perfect hostile complete with original Incan walls for my accommodations.

The staff at my new "home" offered me coca tea and assured me that this would help with the fuzziness and shortness of breath that I must be experiencing after arriving. I felt none. Feeling invincible, I declared myself altitude immune.

The adventure officially began.

Energy emanated from the people, the structures. My own body seemed to buzz, and I kept looking at my feet to make sure that my hiking boots were actually making contact with the ground. It was as if I was a frozen, cryogenic specimen who'd been released from the cold and this multisensory environment acted like a warm heater to help me thaw. A tingling emotional excitement seemed to knit its

63

way into the very cloth that blanketed this place. Great massive walls erected during the Incan Empire were juxtaposed with modern influences and the onslaught of the Spanish Inquisition.

I walked into a tourist agency that had a friendly feel about it.

"Buenos dios!" I said and, between Spanish dictionary words and excited English, I must have appeared confidently illiterate.

In college I was labeled "language deficient" and placed in beginning Spanish to remedy this error. I soon discovered, however, that I was destined for trouble when everyone there attended some high school courses. The college professor spoke the language from the first "hola" and I realized that knowing the birthday song and counting to ten would not get me far.

Now in Peru, despite my checkered bilingual past, I launched into my best speech about adventure and soulsearching. The South American woman's eyes enlarged like that of a deer caught in the headlights.

As my explanation became more controlled, she relaxed and assured me that she spoke a little English.

"I'm here on this quest—a spiritual journey, and there are questions I have about how to get to certain places."

She tried to sell me the deluxe tourist package.

"No, no," I explained. "I'm looking for those experiences that are more or less off the beaten path."

The more we talked the more she registered my intention.

Finally she said, "Ah, who you need is Carmen."

At dawn the next day I waited on the steps of my hostel for the mysterious Carmen.

I had paid the requested soles for her to be my guide for the day and walked away with a small piece of paper as a receipt. It told me what time to be ready and that I would be picked up in front of where I was staying. The time came but no Carmen.

"Was this to be my first foreign rue?" I sighed and began replaying the previous day's events in my head. Perhaps my excitement had precluded better judgment. Just as I was thinking that it didn't even matter whether she came or not, a horn sounded and a hand waved from behind the glare of the windshield.

"Are you David?"

I nodded.

"Get in," she invited.

A dark-haired, round-faced angel sat behind the wheel.

Carmen's vehicle was like some cross-pollination experiment between a car and a van. The front seats held a cinematic view.

Beyond the city limits, we ventured into what is known as the Sacred Valley. Again, without warning, tears came. This time I was more self conscious, for this person I had known less than an hour was about to experience my personal flood.

"Are you alright?" she questioned, patting my knee.

"Yes, yes," I assured her. "It's just that I'm so relieved to be here."

65

That was it! Relief was the sensation that always seemed to come into my life whenever I procrastinated in doing something and then finally just did it. I often wondered what specific fears kept me so immobile?

Carmen remained quiet for awhile and let me cry as I took in the scenery.

I felt so comfortable here.

When my tears slowed, she leaned toward me, breaking the silence. "May I talk to you in that way?"

"What way?" asking the question only in my mind.

"Welcome home," she whispered, smiling.

I felt an electrical charge pass through me.

"When I picked you up in front of your hostel, I was visibly surprised. You have the aura of the Inca. It is huge. We get thousands of seekers and spiritual travelers here every month, but rarely do I see someone whose luminous energy is like that of the ancient ones." I feel as if you are my brother."

This kind of talk didn't shock me, in fact I find myself open to just about anything. Internally, I carried on a verbal dual.

"Yeah, perfect!" I reflected.

Then, a little bit of Southern California cynicism cropped up and shouted, "Oh puuhleazzze, she says that to everybody!"

That less than trusting nature envisioned a well-seasoned guide reciting from a script.

"Welcome home. (yawn) You have the aura of the Inca (yawn). "Is it working? Is he buying it?"

66

I snapped out of the trance and looked at her. She didn't yawn or look at me with a rehearsed expression. Her face glowed.

"I have an idea," she said. "Why don't we do a welcoming home ceremony?"

"Perfect," I responded.

That was exactly the kind of experience I had envisioned and prayed would present itself to me.

We drove for another 32 kilometers to a set of ruins called Pickallachta. The place was deserted. Carmen and I began walking through the delicate towers of earth and stone. Here, archaeologists must have been on some type of excavation, for their tools and make shift tarps indicated their presence. On this day, however, no one was around.

"What's all this?" I questioned.

"Research, excavations, but funding keeps running out."

We climbed over steps and entered a narrow passageway between two towering stone walls.

"Now let's see," she debated, "where can I take you?

She fumbled through her pockets for something.

"Oh, I cannot believe I left my quartz at home," she disappointedly observed. "I never do that."

I reached in my pocket to produce my own.

Back in Los Angeles, heading out the door to the airport, something drew me inside for one last glance around the house. I reviewed every appliance, every window, every everything since I knew it would be awhile before I returned. My eyes kept gazing on the ceremonial altar in my bedroom.

67

Displayed there, was a collection of crystals that I had gathered over the years. One, beautiful, oblong quartz seemed the perfect candidate to go along on the journey.

I held it up for Carmen.

"Excellent!" she cheered, clasping the crystal in her hands. She reached down to the frayed hem of her shawl and pulled out one long thread, tying it around the middle of the crystal.

"Now we will know where to go," she assured and held the thread high above her head as the attached crystal dangled in the air. The sunlight seemed to target it like a champion marksman, piercing it with brilliant rays.

The crystal began to spin.

Its rotation was slow at first and then increased in speed in an acrobatic air dance. When it stopped she studied the direction the point of the crystal faced. "Follow me," she said and navigated the way.

Follow, I did, thinking that compasses were so passe'.

We came upon a little grassy area that seemed to have welcoming home ceremony written all over it.

In my best lotus position, I positioned myself on the ground as Carmen began invoking the spirit of the puma, the snake and the condor, the three elements of the Incan heritage. As she circled and chanted blessings, I closed my eyes, feeling the energy of the place."

In Spanish she recited prayers and continued her melodic chanting, some of which I could understand and some of which I could not. I cheated a little and peeked through the slits in my eyes to watch her sway her arms and lift them to the skies. I loved her spirit, her calm manner. "What a great synchronistic stroke of brilliance to bring us together," I thought.

I closed my eyes fully and breathed in my environment.

Yet, as she went through the ceremony, an unfamiliar phrase resounded in my head, buzzing in a repetitive wave. The phrase was not in English and I assumed that I must be picking up on something that she said in her native tongue. The more I tried to concentrate, breathe, and be, the louder and more forceful the phrase became. It beat upon my brain like a ceremonial tom-tom and I heard and sensed nothing else.

When Carmen completed the ceremony, I opened my eyes and looked at her. She stood directly in front of the sun's rays. Intense backlighting made her appear majestic among the ancient pillars. I readjusted my focus and saw her beaming down at me.

"What does this mean?" I said, repeating the phrase that had reverberated throughout my body.

Her expression changed to shock.

"You did not tell me you spoke Quecha!" she said, as if all this time I had played a game with her and might be masking as an incognito Incan aficionado.

"I don't," I muttered.

Quecha is the true Incan language dating back long before the Spanish Inquisition took place. In fact, most of the indigenous tribes throughout most of South America still speak Quecha to this day.

She continued to stare.

"Really, I don't," I repeated.

"That's Quecha for I am here. I am home!" With that, she grabbed my wrist and said, "We must go see the shaman!"

We peeled out in our best Indiana Jones fashion and headed to God knows where.

"You don't get this in tour packages," I mused as clouds of dust rose from her accelerating tires.

For half an hour she stared and muttered words like "Quecha" and "unbelievable".

I was clueless to my actual whereabouts. Carmen, shamans and South America, all totaled up to be one sweet mystery.

We turned down an unmarked dirt road that opened onto an anonymous village. Half-naked children, chickens and dogs scurried around like frenetic fleas.

Carmen honked the horn and, like the Red Sea, the crowd miraculously parted.

We stopped at a non-descript house-hut. Carmen instructed me to get out and wait by the car.

She walked to the well-worn door and knocked.

A woman with a baby strapped to her back opened the door and stuck her head out. She listened then studied me, trying to match Carmen's story with the figure fidgeting beside the car. Several little heads peeped out from behind the woman. Their appearance seemed choreographed like a vaudevillian opening number. All eyes stared at the funny American. I waved and their giggles drew them back inside.

Up until that moment, I had not met a bona fide,

cardcarrying shaman. I wasn't sure what shaman "proto-col" was and the last thing I wanted to do was offend him.

"Should I bow? Should I kiss his feet? Is there some secret shaman handshake?" I wondered, growing anxious.

Just then, a tiny man stepped outside and greeted Carmen.

He was filthy, his hair matted, his neck, arms and hands streaked with dirt and sweat as if his work in the fields had been abruptly interrupted. My attention was drawn to a simple article of clothing. He wore a sweater vest—you know, like from the Gap!

"Where'd he get it?" Perhaps he put on his finest to greet me? Maybe this was a preview of the fall line from Alpaca R Us? My brain buzzed with fascination and fear.

"Focus, David, focus!" I told myself.

Bouncing like a convention of ping-pong balls, my mind ricocheted between Gap commercials and proper protocol procedures as this little, filthy, but smartly accessorized sha-man approached.

Face to face, I mumbled my most cordial greeting.

He simply stood and stared.

Raising my eyebrows at Carmen, I hoped she would intercede. She didn't.

He continued to stand and stare.

I felt like I was committing some terrible blunder, then came the overwhelming urge to simply stare back. Our eyes met, our gazes locked.

Nowadays, it is a rare treat to have someone's undi-vided attention—to know that beyond a shadow of a doubt

71

that you have one hundred percent of their focus—you are being heard. More than that, you are being honored. The treat was here. I didn't want to miss a moment.

We continued to see each other and my chaotic mind gave way to a tremendous sense of warmth and welcome.

When I caught up to his same level of awareness, he extended his hand and took mine. In Quecha he announced, "Welcome home! Indeed you are the old beloved."

Chills raced through my spine.

My name, David Ault, means old beloved.

He captured my full attention.

The shaman escorted us into his home and sat on a cushion next to an oblong table. He reached into a bag of coca leaves and raised the collection heavenward between his palms. He then scattered them across the table and began to study their pattern.

The next hour was a revelation beyond description.

He spoke softly, and Carmen interpreted. He told of my past incarnations within the Peruvian culture and that this life would bring me back for many continued initiations. He said this trip would only begin to scratch the surface of my true destiny here, but scratch it, it would. I would be forever changed.

Without him knowing I make my living as a professional speaker, he added, "You must tell them that the time for the spirit of the Old Beloved to awaken in all of their hearts is now." He revealed that there is a place within each of us that knows why we are here. It is that ancient and sacred connection that continues to produce the longing within us to answer and greet our destiny. We are to run into its arms and let it carry us to greatness. It is where our spiritual homesickness can dissolve by crossing the threshold of remembrance. All our excuses, our procrastinations, our history must be let go like the seedlings of the dandelion in the wind of the Infinite. As scary and unsure as that action might feel, we will never know true peace unless we allow ourselves to own our uniqueness.

"You've waited many years to sit here with me," he smiled. "I deliver to you nothing you have not heard before. But, I ask you to hear deeper."

I looked up at him and gazed fully into his eyes. They held every invitation to safety and wisdom that my soul was seeking.

"Go and meet your destiny," he urged. "Your council is with you. There are mighty works to be done and the time to begin is now. Do not be afraid."

Had he uttered these final words? No. But I heard and understood.

1) *Are there "calls" in your life that continue to whisper to you, asking you to abandon intellect, reason and opinion? What are they?*

2) *If money, time and circumstance were no option, where would you go for your vision quest?*

3) *What are 5 steps you could do now to help facilitate this vision quest in becoming a reality? Are you willing to begin "flowing your energy" creatively? (i.e. constructing a dreamboard, studying the language if different than your own, begin saving money, getting in physical shape, studying travel books of the area, renting movies or documentaries about your desired destination.)*

Is This Seat Taken?

As long as I can remember, forgiveness has been on the Top Ten List of enlightened activities we are supposed to practice. That list is always headed by love (the greatest of these is…) yet, the value of forgiveness for personal growth seems to edge out other practices like meditation, visualization and getting enough fiber. But, if you bolt the door, draw the curtains and step into the truth booth, most of us would rather ignore forgiveness. We figure that by doing so, maybe we would out grow the need for it.

In that pesky, self-composed concerto entitled *Should*, there's a scratch on the record playing on our mental phonograph. The needle and scratch meet incessantly skipping on the lyric, "we should forgive, we should forgive, we should forgive," and we numbingly put on earmuffs.

(Lest the metaphor be lost on those born later than me,

9-AULT

substitute laser for needle and compact disc for record.)

Most of us would rather get our spiritual "brownie" points from saving the rain forests or helping senior citizens cross the street than to consider forgiveness, much less embrace it, as a way of life. For many, the word forgiveness has a negative, energetic punch to it. It conjures up thoughts of sacrifice, caving in, being a door mat or condoning inexcusable behavior. When we do forgive, we often feel the winds of spiritual superiority wafting from Mt. Righteousness. They blow their message of "Yes, we all know you screwed up, but I, in my infinite enlightenment, forgive you."

Many purchase the forgiveness safety kit that comes with a lock for the heart. It's the perfect accessory for those who say they forgive but add one little security clause, "I forgive you, but I'm keeping my eye on you in case you do it again."

Let's face it, very rarely do any of us run toward the opportunity of forgiveness. It can be immensely challenging to see ourselves and forgiveness galloping towards each other like separated lovers in a field of daisies. Instead, our defenses usually take us on a lead-footed trudge where countless potholes bear the remains of our blood, sweat and resistance.

Forgiving means releasing the grip on the blanket of emotional pain that we've used for why our lives aren't working. It feels like giving up our identity to some witness protection program. How can we continually be asked to give up our justifiable indignation? "It doesn't feel safe," we moan. "Can't you see I'm the victim here?"

My own relationship with forgiveness would falter every time I felt a sense of injustice.

Being the last of five children, I was often the recipient of the overwhelming anxiety my mother felt at being widowed. She was the single parent times five, holding on and trying her best to cope in the never-ending tornado of responsibility. As was typical for that era, parents did not "spare the rod." The belt buckles, bridal wreath branches and anything else within reach were objects magnetized to my skin. I often cried out, "What did I do?" without ever receiving a sensible answer.

Feeling the need for one, I'd make up my own.

"I am a burden, an irritant, and must learn to please more."

Often in my elementary school years, I would save my milk money and purchase my mother's favorite candy bar. The plan would be to place it in the freezer so that when she crawled wearily in from work, there would be a frozen treat, just the way she liked it, a panacea for her despair. I'd come home and vacuum, dust, wash dishes, finish my homework—anything that I could think of to keep her overwhelm from rearing and expressing it's unpredictable head. But the cause for its arrival remained inconsistent. Unable to second-guess what would set her off, I stopped trying and "hid" in school activities or books that helped me voyage to a calmer place.

Belief in injustice stayed with me and I continued to create it over and over again. To forgive who or what was responsible seemed like volunteering to be burned at the stake. I wanted to incite mutiny, to fight back and to gather as many empathetic soldiers as possible for my war against injustice. It felt as though my survival depended on it.

But warring never defeated the demon. It just kept showing up, different city, different face, same feeling of victimization.

I tired of this self-imposed battle but the avenue of forgiveness seemed as effortless as a lead suited swim across the Pacific.

In my counseling, the response when I suggest the practice of forgiveness is as complex as it is amusing. Some go into apoplexy at the mere mention of the word. With others, I can see their inner warrior emerge, willing to embrace the idea, but ready to go down into the muck and the mire for what they believe to be the long, arduous battle.

"Forgiveness is difficult," our internal chatter cries, and, quite predictably, our experiences match our belief. I know mine did.

Because of this, I don't suggest forgiveness anymore.

I advocate understanding.

Imagine that you are facing a row of chairs. On the far left side is the seat reserved for the vilest of criminals. It is where the terrorists, rapists and murderers of the world are assigned seats. Next to them sit their accomplices, the most notorious thieves, arsonist and grifters. Continuing down, we see the ones artful in mental abuse and manipulation. We observe the chronic liars, the ones who abandon and cheat on their spouses. There are the slumlords and the notorious bosses who exercise control like prison wardens. Further right, the heinous crimes against humankind and nature lessen and the seats are filled with struggling alcoholics, food, drug or sex addicts and gamblers. They rub elbows with their neighbors who are frozen in fear, letting their dreams and personal well being gather dust within that neglected place long buried in their heart. Getting closer to the other end, we acknowledge those who are committed to a conscious path, yet still buy in to the world's illusion of hardship and lack. Eventually, we come to the opposite end of the row.

Funny, but in looking at this last seat, the person occupying it doesn't seem to be touching the upholstery at all. The lightness of their being gives the impression of floating. We have journeyed to that unworn chair reserved for those who remember their magnificence, choose only love and embrace everything with an open heart.

This assemblage of remarkably varied individuals is what I call The Row of Human Awareness.

In every occupied seat, the light of truth shines.

In every one?

Yes, in every one. But in those on the far left, that light can be reduced to an almost undetectable flicker.

The flame gathers brilliance and intensity the further we expand our consciousness and remember who we are— ambassadors of love, and what we came here to do—give and receive that love.

So what does this have to do with understanding?

Well, at one time or another *we all have sat in every chair.*

79

"Oh come on," would arise the familiar argument. "I've never murdered anyone or committed any acts of terrorism!"

Yes, but we have all hated.

The catalyst for those extreme acts is an uncompromising hostility fed and fawned over. With time layering that hatred and fossilizing any love to an ancient memory, those occupying the chairs of unspeakable horrors have forgotten what their original mission in this life is, and live hardened by their past.

Our rage and hatred is the exact same feeling, just expressed differently.

Without condoning the behavior, we can look at the original feeling and say, "Yes I have felt that way."

We can understand

From a different vantage point, I could look at all my mother faced during those years and identify with her overwhelm and escalation of fear. It was her way of dealing with survival. She had to provide for the family on a secretary's salary, keeping food and shelter over our heads. The odds seemed stacked against her. Yet, somehow, she managed to keep us off the streets. Do I wish she had been able to accomplish this in a Donna Reed/June Cleaver sort of way? Of course, but she did it in the only way she was familiar.

We can look at any given seat and identify with the occupants' fears, feelings of unworthiness, guilt or shame. There may even be those whose life choices match our own.

Understanding the feeling behind the actions, we view those who have acted out against us in a different light. This approach retrains us to see the behavior for what it is, the misdirected action from an old wound, the root cause undoubtedly traced to childhood trauma and suffering.

Several years ago, a great uncle revealed to me how abusive my grandmother had been to my mom. The restrictions placed on her helped shut down a little girl once bursting with creativity and humor. Clearly we act out the same script, generation after generation. Understanding can rewrite the pages that influence our performance.

Repeatedly, the simplicity of this approach is met by opposition. In this vast, human playground, our conditioning has taught us to blame. Without hesitation, we are ready to verbally attack, emotionally punish and withhold love at the slightest provocation. None of us like being the bulls eye of emotional or physical arrows aimed at us by reactive marksmen, but how many times a day do we pick up our own bow, dust off the arrows and do a little misguided archery ourselves? Over time, I have released my own fair share of angry arrows but the path of personal responsibility has led me to put down my emotional weaponry and look at my choices. I can embrace understanding, be open to the lesson and move on, or blame and create a life filled with malevolent destructive energy.

We know the latter choice fertilizes the weeds in the garden of our lives. Yet, we've all dug in our heels, bloody knuckled our grip and refused to change. Refusing to understand and then forgive chokes the sweet breath of life from us.

I continue to be fascinated by my own trek through the fields of understanding and forgiveness. What I thought

81

was an issue long since resolved could pop up in my head, starting a chain reaction of memories lasting for far too long.

Recently, while driving, I recalled someone I had not thought of or heard from in at least ten years. I remembered her as lighthearted, gregarious and fun. That led to a memory of getting together with her and a group of others for a social occasion. I brought along my partner at the time, making introductions and meeting the others at the party that were new to me. At dinner I was seated next to the lighthearted woman and enjoyed the banter and the laughter considerably. On the ride home with my partner, the mood changed. He ridiculed my behavior and was considerably dismayed at the lack of attention I had shown his way. It was a no win discussion. Regardless of how many times I tried to bring him into the conversation, he was not satisfied. Having this replay in my mind, I conjured up anger over a ten-year old incident! That sense of injustice was still a very active bee pollinating my belief system. I thought I was done with that chapter of my life and had done all of the releasing neces- sary. Apparently not.

This example sheds awareness on the fact that all of us spend a great deal of our waking hours chaining one angry memory to the next. We lose track of just how much time is spent there. By the end of the day, we're dragging the im- measurable chains of our anger and wondering why we feel so weighted down by life. We go to bed only to start the process over again the following morning—day after day, year after year. Is it any wonder that alarming numbers of individuals suffer from depression, anxiety, and the accompanying illnesses these mental states provide?

Realizing where I was headed, I stopped dragging the chain of thoughts and explored understanding my former partner's reaction. He had chosen a torturous road filled with every imaginable hurdle to self-worth one could muster. He trail-blazed a path to loathing that years together had revealed. I needed to examine my issues of rescuing; he needed to make peace with his past. It was obvious that I could not fix anything even though he professed to want me to. It was a union wrapped in disharmony and resentment. It was my relationship with my mother all over again, and I had shown up to make someone else's happiness my responsibility.

Aware of this now, I could make the choice to understand his reaction on that drive home and see how his fear could make him lash out. I could choose peace.

Understanding will always be the wayshower to fulfilling our longing for peace. We crave peace like a baby craves milk, and the Universe is forever trying to feed us. Continuing to blame creates a cycle of throwing the bottle to the ground and expecting others to pick it up. The people pleasers will want to rescue the bottle to appease the blamers, and the exhausting treadmill of dysfunction begins.

Gerald Jampolsky, the beloved physician, author and founder of The Center For Attitudinal Healing has spent a great deal of his life applying the principles of forgiveness and understanding to his own experiences. His personal path, research and client testimonials offer forgiveness as the number one healer of every illness we could possibly

83

imagine. I believe that ranking to be accurate, it's effects sustainable, when that act of forgiveness is blended with feeling good about the choice. How we feel about our decision will directly influence the result. If we go through the motions of forgiveness because it's the noble thing to do—our spiritual leaders assign it, yet feel resentful about it, the results will be limiting at best. But, if we wait for a time when we are feeling good—laughing, in a setting of bliss, and then do our forgiveness work, the energetic tone of that sacred act will produce the rhapsodic inner harmony we all long for.

Blending forgiveness with a feeling of joy would sort of make it the elixir of life, wouldn't it?

If we were offered such an elixir as the healing agent of our malaise, wouldn't we gladly drink?

Refusing to understand or forgive is like taking that precious vial and tossing it away.

We have the power to stop the repeated patterns and change our lives back to the vibrancy of a child. As my friend Maureen calls it, that place within us that has never been violated.

First, define what seat you are residing in on the Row of Awareness and begin to provide a bit of self-directed compassion. Choose the power of understanding to forgive the past and appreciate the journey that got you this far. Honoring everything as a divine teacher helps unlock the chains that restrict freedom, liberating us from mental and emotional imprisonment. This freedom gives wings to your pain. Release it with love and be done.

Second, of everyone else you encounter, stop and consider the question.

"What chair is he or she sitting in?" Know, too, that you have been there yourself and watch the softening of your actions create a better way.

The more I chose to understand my mother's life, the faster I regained the true essence of mine.

With dutiful intention, you may find yourself moving to the end of the row, unaware that you seem to be floating above an unworn cushion.

1) What feelings arise when you are presented with the topic of forgiveness?

2) Are there some individuals whom you feel would be too difficult to forgive? Would you be willing to examine their behavior, their life issues and circumstances, to see if there was a way to develop understanding for their actions?

3) In regards to the people you interact with, silently practice asking the question, "I wonder what seat they are sitting in?" Then follow that with the awareness, "I, too, have sat in that chair. Therefore, I can understand why they would respond the way they have."

Stand Up, Jean Louise,
Your Father's Passing

Reflecting on the cinema's power to influence, I often wonder why more directors, writers, and producers aren't using their talents to create movies that raise social conscience, inspire, or educate.

Not that there aren't those movies out there, but the ratio of what the public is offered seems to weigh heavily on the violent or innocuous side of the cinematic seesaw.

Call me old-fashioned, but I get caught up in the stories of redemption, bravery, and love conquering all.

I have a soft spot, too, for films that have some kind of father influence intertwined in the story telling.

Having lost my dad early on, my eyes start their water works whenever I watch the movie, *Field Of Dreams*. When Kevin Costner's character greets the ghost of his father on

87

the baseball field for a game of catch, his connection with his dad produces a deep longing within *me* for what might have been in my life. How great would it be to have my dad come back from the beyond to participate in an activity that is mutually loved?

In Carl Sagan's book and movie of the same name, *Contact*, the little girl's whole world is wrapped up in her father, only to have him die unexpectedly of heart trouble.

Her misguided guilt in taking responsibility for his death sends her to her ham radio to try and contact him from the constellations—stars he had taught her to appreciate.

These movies chisel away at the hardened walls of my adulthood, and I am always left with the vulnerable side effects.

But, the single most profound film in my grab bag of favorites is *To Kill A Mockingbird*. That whole Southern influence rings true with my Southeast Texas upbringing.

Harper Lee's Pulitzer Prize winning novel and subsequent film adaptation is a testament to purity and integrity—a valentine to values that, today, are more challenging to come by.

In the film, Atticus Finch defends a black man accused of raping a white woman. Being Caucasian, his choice to do so is unthinkable in the depression era South, and he comes under enormous ridicule from his community, inciting threats to him and his family.

Nevertheless, he does his job; one, because he believes in the innocence of his client, and two, because his core values, deeply rooted, support his refusal to sit back and allow bigotry to shine without a fight.

As brilliant as his defense is, he loses the case.

I can identify.

As "brilliant" as my defense is in regard to my life choices, there are times when I "appear to lose the case." I say "appear" because what I may term as loss is actually a blessing in disguise.

"Losing" my father created, by far, the greatest imprint in the pliable mold of my emotional psyche. It shaped how I acted and what I sought after to fill the void after his death.

The amount of attention I got when I returned to second grade after all of the funeral proceedings were over was significant. The teacher made an announcement about my father's death and for weeks, everyone in my class treated me special. The attention was addicting. I craved it, too, because there wasn't much being doled out at home.

But with time, the curiosity of the students returned to normal, and I was left with the unresolved craving.

I'm thankful that I had teachers and other adult influences challenging me to take those cravings and channel them into creative outlets. The feeling of acceptance seemed solely intertwined with performing. Music helped feed the need. School and church became my audition terrain. These were the places where I felt the most loved. Is it any wonder, then, that "extracurricular" became my new middle name? Home was just a place to sleep.

What I have come to understand all these years later is that the death of my father, that loss, actually gave way to the birth of me finding my creative self. My desire for acceptance helped squeeze me out of a restrictive cocoon, forcing me to spread my adolescent wings and fly into uncharted territory. Dad's departure actually acted as a welcome mat to a life-long passion for musical and theatrical expression.

Atticus' loss weighs heavy on him as he leaves the courtroom. But, in a touching display of respect, he unknowingly gets a silent, standing ovation from the black townsfolk in the balcony. His own children, having crept into the balcony to watch the proceedings, fall asleep and are thus awakened by the minister. He gently says, "Stand up, Jean Louise, your father's passing."

To me, it is an unparalleled moment on celluloid depicting the purity and goodness that shines when honoring our basic core values. That crowd in the balcony is so touched by his efforts on behalf of one of their own, that they stand as he passes below. They acknowledge him regardless of how the court ruled. Yet, Atticus is totally unaware of this and walks out feeling heavy-hearted and defeated.

The scene illustrates that we are winners regardless of what the world of the physical might dictate. Our pure intent will always be met with victory. But that victory just might come in a different form than we expected.

How many times have we walked away from a situation feeling defeated, forgetting that the Universe is always standing in our honor? There is that inner voice saying, "We're standing up because you are passing. You deserve it. You are worthy."

There is so much magic in that moment for me—a collection of all that is pure and filled with integrity, loss, and victory—the full spectrum of life.

On a recent speaking trip in Winnipeg Manitoba, I drove by a theatre in their downtown area and stopped abruptly when I saw the marquee. In big letters read the title *To Kill A Mockingbird.*

"How great to see it on the big screen!" I thought.

It turned out it wasn't the film version at all, but the first stage production adapted from the novel. Excited, I purchased a mezzanine ticket, second row center, for that very night.

It was an exceptional performance. Many parts of the novel that never made it to the film version came alive. The cast was brilliant and the sets and direction first rate.

I anticipated my favorite moment, but with no balcony on stage, I wondered how it would be directed or if it would be cut from the production.

The second act started, and the trial ran its course. Sitting so still, the only things moving were my lips that silently mouthed the dialogue.

Atticus is defeated and prepares to leave.

"This is it," I thought.

Suddenly actors placed in the front row began to slowly stand.

A voice among them said, "Stand up, Jean Louise. Your father's passing."

Right in front of me was my favorite moment being played out in live theatre!

I'm not sure what took over me but I stood as well! It

was as if a will greater than my own raised me up before I could rationalize my way out of it. I *needed* to stand, to recognize truth—the truth of the character on stage as well as my own—to stand and honor a Divine plan much greater than my human abilities can sometimes grasp. I was *participating* in this long beloved moment, and I was overcome with awe.

I found deep connection in that act—connection with why I love that story so much. Atticus is the father I wished for but never physically had. That longing propelled me to a relationship with the all knowing, all loving Father whose unwavering faith and belief in me is the blueprint for all the Atticus' that ever were and ever will be.

That night, as I slept in a strange city in a different country, I felt close to my dad. It was as if he had graced me with his presence and given me the cue that he was with me—standing, honoring, watching, and guiding.

Over the years I've wondered if my father is guiding me in my day to day decisions. I look for signs and often ask questions of him. And, there are times when he seems to be responding; his presence known in ways tinged with humor and magic.

How?

Well, the simplest objects can be ways of saying hello.

I have always had this uncanny knack for finding pennies on the ground wherever I am—even in foreign countries. I find them on the street, sidewalks, restaurant floors, in rental cars—just about every conceivable surface—pennies for the taking. Once outside the walled city of Luca in

Italy, there lay an American penny in a patch of clover.

I was sharing being a penny magnet with my brother Daniel when he smiled and reflected on our dad.

"You were too young or maybe not even born yet," he said "but Dad had the neighborhood children convinced that our front yard was magic."

"How?" I asked.

"Because there were always coins in the clover patches of our front yard. At first, even I thought it was magic, until one day I saw dad standing in the yard among us—his hand slowly coming out of his pockets dropping coins inconspicuously onto the ground."

I had to laugh. My brother's story was dad's confirmation, letting me know that he *was* dropping in on me and checking on my welfare. Even though I was not around yet for the treasure in the yard, I was getting my turn. Every coin I now find becomes a rousing hello from him!

Dad **is** there whether I am on foreign soil or filling my car with gasoline. Those pennies are my signals that his presence is real. They are pennies from heaven.

At the start of my high school years my mother married Sam, a man from our church. He was very kind and able to provide my mother things that she never had before. The household was nothing elaborate but it was a far cry from what we experienced as children on her secretary's salary.

Sam taught me to drive, took me on my first water-skiing outing, and showed me how to really shine a shoe. It was mom and Sam who came to my graduations and sent me off to New York to be an aspiring actor.

93

They were married 25 years, and the family recently returned to Beaumont to honor their silver wedding anniversary. There were quite a number of jokes told about how many times Sam had to ask my mother to marry before she said yes. She teased back, denying the whole thing.

Just six weeks after the celebration, Sam went out for his usual early morning walk. It was August and the days held the kind of sticky, humid conditions that make Texas resemble a hissing boiler room. Because of the heat, he left the house to walk in the cooler, pre-dawn hours. He didn't return.

Mother became worried. After all, it was Sunday, and he should have been home showering and getting ready for church hours ago.

My oldest sister Brenda happened to be visiting that weekend because of a family wedding. My mother went to wake her and tell her of her concern.

They got in the car to search the neighborhood finding police cars just a block away. They seemed to be cleaning up the remains of an accident.

It involved Sam.

My mother identified Sam's watch and the officer informed her that he had been hit at an impact calculated at nearly 60 miles an hour. It was a hit and run just down the street from the house he lived in for over 40 years—a walk he had taken countless mornings through every season of the calendar.

It is hard to describe that week as he lay on life support. They worked tirelessly to determine if he had any brain activity, but test after test revealed that there was not. The decision to remove him from the respirator was made and Sam passed away—another father figure gone.

It dawned on me at the service that Sam, more or less, took care of our mother for 25 years. Because of that, my brothers, sisters, and I chose opportunities in other states or cities, and we got to experience our lives without having to worry about our mother. Sam had given us a tremendous gift. How different would my life have been if my mother had never remarried?

Now, with my mom in her 80s and unable to drive, I fly back and forth from California to Texas, helping handle the never-ending to-do lists.

On one such visit, I painted the interior of her house.

While taking a breather outside, away from the paint fumes, I relaxed on the wrought iron bench under the porch area and looked out onto the street. I thought about what it must have been like for my father to be a paint contractor. "You look just like him," my sister Brenda commented, seeing me after a day's laboring, paint droplets covering my hair and face with cream-colored freckles. Like my father, this certainly wasn't my one and only experience with a brush. To supplement my income as an actor, I painted my share of walls from New York to Los Angeles.

Scraping the drops of paint off my fingernails, I noticed a black pencil sitting beside me on the bench. It was one of those mechanical ones adorned with a miniature 8 ball on the top.

It read, *"Before you get behind the 8 ball on your paint-*

95

ing and decorating, call Pete Ault – phone 41271." finishing with our address. It was my dad's pencil, advertising his paint contracting business!

The pencil had to be over 45-50 years old! How did it get there? This wasn't the house that he and my mother lived in together. I stared at the pencil for what seemed an eternity, paint-covered fingers caressing an object familiar with being held that way. Had it been magically placed there for my benefit?

Dazed, I took it inside to show my mother. She couldn't imagine where the pencil came from either but remembered dad using them as promotion.

The pencil just *appeared*, something far more specific than a penny.

It was as if my dad was acknowledging my taking care of mom, painting as he had, and in an obtuse way, telling me it was time to start my writing.

With this chapter on fathers, I used that mechanical pencil to edit and make changes—dad being a part of his own tribute.

Several weeks after Sam's funeral, I stood before a congregation in Virginia giving the Sunday morning lesson. As I looked out over the audience, I couldn't help but notice a woman in the front row busy with pen and paper. She would stare in my direction and then return to writing. My first thought was that she was simply taking notes, but there was a fervency about it that made me curious.

After the service, paper in hand, she walked up to me.

"While you were speaking, she explained, I saw images of two older men, one on either side of you. They both rested a hand on your shoulder and simply smiled as you spoke. It felt as though they were standing with you, acknowledging and supporting you as you continue choosing a path towards enlightenment. I just had to write it down because there was such peace about them."

Curious, I asked her if she could tell me what they looked like.

"Certainly," she replied and began describing my father Pete and my stepfather Sam quite accurately.

I realized in that moment that "loss" is relative. What we cannot hold or taste or touch in the physical does not mean it isn't there. We have the opportunity to realize that the nonphysical, and all its intuitive and spiritual gifts make up a much greater part of our experience than what we can actually see.

Atticus may have never known the silent honor given him by the Alabama townsfolk. Pete and Sam seem intent on giving me a different experience.

1) *What would you consider to be the most significant losses in your life?*

2) *In hindsight, can you see how these perceived losses brought about a new direction or clarity of purpose?*

3) *The Universe is always "standing up" in your honor, acknowledging you for the simple act of being. Have there been times when you were aware of this supportive power of acknowledgment?*

All That (And a Bag of Chips)

On Fridays, when the 3:10 bell rang to announce the end of school, the sweet taste of freedom joined with another taste, the traditional cheeseburger. In tandem, a dozen or so of my fellow classmates from James Bowie Junior High School would set our collective intentions and our bicycle tires towards The Burger Joynt. The coins I earned from scavenging and returning pop bottles jingled in my pockets as I pedaled my bike. My friends Chuck and Randy's own collection—Chuck's from an actual allowance, Randy's from an early morning paper route which contributed to his head drooping in second period English, joined mine in announcing our youthful presence. There was a musicality to the coins, far more satisfying than the rapid percussive cadence from playing cards we sometimes pinned to our spokes. It was Friday—our entire bodies, attitude and countenance

99

sang out freedom.

Down Steelton and Monroe Ave, we crossed over to Magnolia Blvd. where a sidewalk ran parallel with the road. We steered with one hand and reached up to grab the leaves off the low-lying branches of the trees that had given the street its name.

Mr. Fitzgerald, the owner of this innocuous little fast food stand, stood faithfully behind the glass in front of the grill. Expecting his posse of eleven and twelve-year-olds, he'd already started to prepare for our out-of-breath arrival.

On Fridays, when we ordered the Burger Basket Special, Fitzy (as we kids affectionately nicknamed him) would always surprise us with something extra. One week, it might be a deluxe order of Cajun spiced french fries, another week a root beer float, or my personal favorite—a super-sized bag of Wise BBQ potato chips. The chips contained so much red dye number four that the stained tips of my fingers could believably pass in show and tell as the hands from a massacre.

I loved the element of surprise, the not knowing in Fitzy's burger presentations as he showed gruff amusement in our faithful visits. I cherished the months when nature cooperated and allowed us to eat at the weathered picnic table outside the stand.

Over time, the bicycle gave way to a beat up Toyota Celica, but I still managed to pay a visit to Fitzy every now and then. Instead of at the picnic table, it was now socially hip to eat inside one's car. With a burger basket on my lap, the radio blaring *Captain Fantastic and the Brown Dirt Cowboy* by

Elton John, I ate and dreamed of the day when the rest of the world would open its door, and I'd run unabashedly through it.

I figured this town had taught me everything it could, and there were no more answers to be found here. I was ready to be inspired. I was longing for instruction, a map to help heal my spiritual homesickness.

Thinking that the answers awaited in some mysterious future, I missed the answers in the present moment. Even the man flipping burgers was a true spiritual teacher—a Zen master of sorts.

In Zen wisdom, there are three simple principles that parallel many other spiritual philosophies:

1) We each have an inner spark—a passionate dream or purpose that beckons us to explore bringing it to life. And, we already possess the attributes to make that purpose a reality.

2) We must go about doing the work—putting one foot in front of the other toward the fulfillment of that purpose.

3) We must give up how it has to happen.

Giving up the "how" seems to be the greatest stumbling block for any spiritual seeker. The third step requires us to lose our rigidity in how we expect our good to appear. Fitzy taught me that when I commit to showing up for what I want (the burger basket), when I produce the money that I earned to pay for it, then I can relax, sit back and know that I will be delivered what I ordered and possibly receive something even greater. I will get all that—and a bag of chips.

Unless, of course, I carry within me the piranha to faith—

101

worry. Worry is that insatiable energy that feeds on our faith and trust, never allowing the peace of surrender to see the light of day.

I know. I come from a long line of championship worriers. When my father's death dramatically changed the family dynamic, I immersed myself in a sense of responsibility uncharacteristic to a boy of seven. Always wanting to go the extra mile and leave behind some semblance of excellence, I decided that I could not do that unless I worried about the outcome. All the people in my immediate world practiced worry. My mother worried over basic survival for the family, my siblings worried about everything from marriage and jobs to grades and school romances. My teachers worried about the continued outbreak of encephalitis from the mosquitoes. The local news told us to worry about hurricanes in the late summer and fall, to worry about being mistaken for a buck once deer season opened, and then there was the mother of all worries—racial unrest. The way people talked, it was a storm as fierce as a class 4 or 5 hurricane about to whip through our desegregated backyards. Life, thy companion is worry.

From what I saw, to be responsible meant that you worry—plain and simple. If you weren't worrying about every detail then somehow you were careless and non-committal. Worry and responsibility became enmeshed like the tiny wires of a screen door—indistinguishable where one or the other begins and the other leaves off.

When the first round of a chronic cough started in the fall of 2000, I knew I was going to have to explore making changes in my work situation. I had difficulty with my voice and experienced the humbling that comes when unable to perform at a level I was used to delivering.

Walking through the Dallas/Ft Worth airport to make a connection, I wondered if this might be my last trip for awhile. As the careerist in me seemed to chant *Dead Man Walking*, a bright fluorescent advertisement grabbed my attention. In bold letters it simply read *Embrace Change*, followed by a description for some banking institution. I wish I could say that at that moment, transformation occurred as the heavens opened and a choir of angelic voices began to triumphantly sing *The Hallelujah Chorus*. It was the exact opposite. I felt anger rising from my gut, and I was tempted to take my shoe off and hurl it at the sign.

"What do you want from me, God?" I pleaded. "I thought I was following my call? If I can't speak and sing then who am I?"

Back at home, I stared at the stack of unpaid bills that were collecting on my desk. My responsible self picked them up and began to spread them out across the length of my dining room table. I have a *big* dining room table. Viewing my papered horizon, worry stepped in to join its responsible companion. I had no idea where the money for the month's expenses was going to come from. The cough had cleared my calendar.

I sat reverting to a form of prayer that involved bargaining with God.

"If you get me out of this, if you make this cough go away, I promise I'll do whatever you want. I'll dig ditches, devote my life to the preservation of the rain forest...etc."

The pile of papers closest to the table's edge fell to the floor startling me out of my trance.

What was I doing? I knew better than to use prayer as a way of beseeching God. My spiritual path had brought to me the revelation of affirmative prayer—the recognition that God is all there is; the unifying belief that if that is so, then I am one *with* God. I took a deep breath and began moving through to the realization that this life already is the thing or experience I want. I gave thanks for the answer and released my prayer.

As I sat in the stillness, the most bizarre question popped into my head.

"Where did your mother pay her bills?"

"What?" I mentally answered.

"Where did your mother pay her bills?"

Going with the question, I thought for a moment and replied, *"at the dining room table."*

"And how was she feeling when she did it?"

That was easy. *"With a sense of worry and panic,"* I answered.

I suddenly realized that I was faithfully carrying on the family tradition.

But how do I break the cycle?

"I don't care how hard you work," the voice continued.

"I beg your pardon?" I moaned, getting a bit indignant.

"I don't care how hard you work. I don't care about the actions you take or the words that you speak. In fact, I don't care about the life path you choose. All I care about is how you feel

when you do them."

I was being called upon to change my approach to my ritualistic choices.

I gathered up the bills and placed them in a large manila envelope. I grabbed my keys, the envelope, and my regained intention and headed to the nearby park. I drove to the most pristine area I could find, parked the car, and started walking toward a secluded picnic bench.

Settling in, I began to look around me at all the abundance nature had on display. There were countless birds darting in circular motions, traveling from treetop to treetop and singing their various theme songs. Not one of them stopped and questioned, *"Am I singing OK? Am I in tune? Cause if I'm not, I'll go back to my nest and rehearse more."* The grass was an endless carpet of green that stretched in all directions. It wasn't feeling the need to justify its existence by commenting, *"Yeah, I know you think I'm green but you should have seen me two springs ago. I was really green."*

All around me there were immeasurable examples of abundance from the hillside rocks, to the granules of earth and the immense blanket of sky. None of them complaining. None of them worrying. They simply were doing their thing; they were fulfilling their purpose without question or justification.

As I sat there, drinking it all in, I began to feel better. Trust was replacing the low-level panic that had churned in my stomach for days and I was able to reconnect with a sense of gratitude. I was consciously changing how I felt. No longer sitting at a table covered with a stockpile of worry,

I had chosen a different table—one that entertained the same element of surprise and appreciation I felt as a young boy at Fitzy's. Reaching into the envelope, I pulled out a bill and wrote out the check for the requested amount. It didn't mean I had the money in my account, but I was inviting the possibility from a place of genuine gratitude and "acting as if." I pulled out another and wrote the check and another and another. When a particularly large bill was extracted, I stopped and redirected my energy back to my surroundings. I waited until I felt appreciative once more and then wrote out that check.

On and on the process went until every bill had its corresponding check for payment. I scooped up the pile of papers, put them back in the envelope, and made my way toward home.

Maneuvering the key in the front door, I heard the telephone begin to ring.

"Hello?"

"Is this David Ault?"

"Yes."

"This is Screen Actors Guild. We're calling to verify your address."

"What for?"

"It shows that a movie you were in several years ago just got bought for video distribution and so we have to go back and pay the actors."

There had been many film projects where salaries had been deferred. There was always the hope that some day,

the film would be bought, and there would be an u̇
paycheck.

"How much?" I questioned.

The woman from membership quoted a figure wit̤
twenty dollars of the amount of checks I had just written in
the park!

Shifting my energy about the bill paying process shifted
my demonstration.

When we recognize that our connection to the Universal Divine presence is based on unconditional love, then we
begin to consider that what we keep getting from life is what
we give back. If we are worriers by nature, then the Universal dialogue goes something like, "Ah, I see you are worrying about paying your bills this month. I love you so much.
Let me give you more bills to worry about. If we are critical
and prone to judgment, it follows that we will be given more
people and circumstances to be critical and judgmental
about. The pessimistic and negative vibrations that we dwell
in will meet and invite those compatible vibrations into our
daily playground.

The same holds true when we vibrate faith, reverence
and joy. When we choose to shift our energy, and consciously court the presence of the Infinite, we recognize that
our frame of mind can display works of freedom rather than
worry, inexhaustible supply over lack. Our Creator equally
matches our vibrational choices.

Most of us walk around unconscious to what we are
vibrating. A bill comes and we immediately think, "Damn,

I'll never get ahead." Our hearts get broken and we declare, "I'll never, *ever* get over this. No one will ever be able to match what they had to offer." We launch a project but inwardly declare, "This is garbage. No one will care." On and on the vibration of despair emanates from us, and we grow accustomed to its presence. Shifting our belief takes recognition of our deeper desire to be willing to change the unconscious, negative routine into a conscious pursuit of positive light-heartedness. Shifting our belief demands we give up our attachment to how our good shows up.

I would have never guessed that money from a movie filmed years before would make its way to me. Letting go of how my good had to appear and shifting my point of power from worry to appreciation opened the channel for a positive demonstration.

So I was able to do it that one time. What about the cough that was effecting my work? The sense of futility was all-pervasive, and I could not seem to find anything about it to appreciate. It was a huge relief to have the current batch of bills paid. But, what about next month? An answer was out there. Would I be willing to let go of the need to control how it appeared?

I made a few phone calls and sent out a few e-mails to friends and contacts telling them that things in my life were changing. I needed a job. Within hours, my friend John called. John is an executive at a large HMO, working as a manager within a large complex information technology department for health plan operations. He asked me if I could come to his office the next day.

The following afternoon, I sat next to the tinted windows overlooking the freeway and listened to his offer. He needed someone to help his project managers stay on top of all the financial paperwork that was required for the various application systems they were implementing. When he asked, "Would you like the job?" I replied, "John, I have no idea what you are talking about. It's as if you are speaking a foreign language." He laughed. "Welcome to corporate America!"

The next few days found me stationed in a cubicle. As I sat there, grasping for clues in how to perform the roles of my job, I was overcome with an enormous sense of failure.

For close to two decades, I made most of my living from my creative endeavors, and here I was sitting between a sea of portable walls attempting to master a job for which I had no passion. Where had I failed?

Day after day, week after week, I sat, coughed, asked questions and tried to live up to John's expectations. I began to get familiar with my duties. After my first month, I realized that the amount of work that was expected of me did not always fill an eight-hour day. There were afternoons with an hour or two where I sat with my thoughts and contemplated my future. I realized that for the first time in well over 15 years, I had a set routine. I was home most nights and weekends. I was cooking and eating my own food. I was resting more. As the sign so many months before had charged, I was embracing change.

Inevitably, my mind would wander to the question, "Now what?" always followed by the answer, "write."

For years, my greatest fantasy was to write a book about my spiritual journey, but a lifestyle of constant travel made the idea a daunting task at best. I also wished for a big time publisher to pay me an advance and whisk me off to the illusive cabin in the woods. There I could produce my version of *Walden Pond*. Amid crisp autumn mornings and a crackling fire, I would pour out my soul to a waiting world.

Okay, there's been no cabin, but for a few hours here and there I surrendered to the writing process at my work cubicle or makeshift office/kitchen table at home. There was no major publisher, but there was an HMO providing a paycheck that allowed me to put off the travel for awhile and become focused at the task of writing my book.

Eventually, my feelings of failure were replaced by sweet surrender. I let go of the limited possibility of how I thought this book should be birthed and set about the task of simply doing the work. My fantasy became a reality; it just took a different route. The gift wasn't wrapped in the shiny paper with the color-coordinated bow—it came in the form of a cough, a mundane job and some much needed solitude.

Hindsight provided me with appreciation. I could actually move into a place of being genuinely thankful for the changes, recognizing the perfection in every aspect of the journey. Perhaps if I saw that illumined airport sign again today, there might even be a few hallelujahs discernible to my tuned-in, tapped-on hearing.

I work at living in that state of appreciation as much as

possible, freeing myself from the ceaseless "how's" of life. When I do, it's like I'm at Fitzy's window all over again. I get all that I've desired and so much more. I get all that and a bag of chips.

1) Many of us shut off the possibility of demonstration in our lives by thinking that our "good" can only manifest in certain ways or through certain people. Can you see that by giving up how it has to appear, that we open ourselves to limitless opportunity? Where in your own life could you be more flexible with the "how" concept?

2) How big a part does worry play in your life? By channeling that energy into flowing appreciation, the need for worry can be replaced by faith in a divine order. Make a list of activities that make you feel appreciative (i.e. being in nature, music, journaling, animals) and commit to mindfully replacing those worry thoughts with acts of gratitude. The results will be remarkable.

3) Finish the sentence, "By embracing change, I can let go of the need to_____ and open up to _____."

Great Wall

Boarding the plane, I felt an ambiguous mix of elation and anxiety.

I have worked in the field of self-empowerment for many years, using storytelling, ceremony, workshops, and music to create an atmosphere of safety and love. All of it is designed to nudge people gently back to a place of remembering their personal divinity and purpose.

But this was a totally new arena. Now I was beginning a flight to Beijing.

All that gentle nudging was to take place on foreign soil away from the comforts and venues that I had previously worked.

With 25 other travelers in tow, I was facilitating a 12-day excursion through the majestic land of China. We would, of course, have English-speaking guides in each of the three cities we were visiting—Beijing, Xian and Shanghai—but my duty, as host/facilitator, was to be the glue that held this trip together.

Saying yes to this opportunity seemed like a natural progression in the continual reinvention of my ministry. Yet, as the roar of the engines announced our ascent, something else announced its presence as well—the voice of self-imposed limitation.

"What do you think you're doing?" it taunted, and for the many traveling hours that carried me over the International Date Line, I could not seem to come up with a reasonable answer.

How many times had I been at this you can do it/no, you can't crossroads in my life? Truthfully, more times than I could give a number to.

There is that space in thought, after the idea has been presented and before its implementation that can be sheer terror. The fear of the unknown and what-ifs creates a battle of worry that leave their mental affliction. Becoming paralyzed by the fear deepens the wound. Facing the fear sheds light on its illusional hold and bit by bit, the sores of inadequacy get bathed by times healing ointment.

Marilyn Ferguson, best-selling author of The Aquarian Conspiracy once wrote, "It's not so much that we're afraid of change or so in love with the old ways, but it's that place in between that we fear…It's like being between trapezes. It's Linus when his blanket is in the dryer. There's nothing to hold on to."

Trying something totally new can feel like grasping for

an invisible trapeze without a safety net. With this trip, the weight of responsibility and possibility of failure loomed large. I needed to face my fear.

I got out of my seat and paced the aisles of the airplane. I began to pick out, one by one, those who were part of my tour—their big yellow buttons with the imprinted China logo helped me identify them. They all seemed so peaceful as they slept.

Then I saw Angela. Several months before the trip, she called me from Albuquerque. She said she was definitely joining the tour and was wondering if she could bring a friend along—a friend who is blind.

I did not know how to answer her and decided to check in with the tour agency to see if they had any restrictions.

"No, there are not any restrictions, but why would a blind person want to go on a sightseeing tour?" they asked.

I admit the same question crossed my mind.

Angela had assured me that she would be with her friend every step of the way so there would be no interruptions for the rest of the group. It seemed a bit crazy, but with her encouragement I was willing to try it.

Now, here they sat next to one another—Angela and her friend Christine. Both women were wide-awake, chatting with radiant smiles. Their enthusiasm made them look uncharacteristically youthful under the glare of airline lighting.

"Thank you for this opportunity!" Christine said as she held out her hand toward the sound of my hello.

"Glad to have you along, "

Shaking her hand, I muttered, "See you when we land."

She smiled. Her cordial response simply, "See you then."

I walked down the aisle momentarily embarrassed. Should I have chosen my words more carefully? How could I have used the word see?

I had visions of the special effects on the television show Ally McBeal taking over, my tongue uncoiling in an embarrassing twisted heap on the floor.

I returned to my seat, my cheeks stinging a bit from the faux pas.

My mind drifted as I thought about Christine. She did not seem to let her blindness limit her. Why was I limiting myself?

I remembered a passage from the Science of Mind® textbook written by the wonderful metaphysician, Ernest Holmes, that said: "Spirit never fails." Never being the key word here—yet I could list column after column of experiences where I had felt failure.

Staring out into the night sky, I was confident that the pilots would navigate us toward our desired destination. Could God's loving guidance be any less accurate? I began to get clear on the difference between Spirit and being human. Our humanness, as the small self, experiences or creates the negative mental dance that comes with failure because oftentimes we believe in it—we expect it. Our Spirit—our divine nature or big Self never fails because It knows of the constancy of creation. It is part of the omniscient, universal whole which can only demonstrate perfection. So with my mental, divine tracing paper, I set out to redraw and replace my belief about my capabilities, moving from human frailty back to spiritual invincibility.

We may go through mountains of tracing paper if we've believed in failure as a given. How many sheets had Christine gone through to get to where she was now? How much mental retraining did it take for her to set her sights grander than what the world told her she was capable of?

I breathed in and focused on the loyalty of Spirit and invited Truth to take over. The possibilities of what this trip could bring began to pulsate within me. Inexplicably, I knew something great was at work, that we had all been assembled like an exuberant marching band led by a synchronistic wave of Spirit's baton. And, I could trust indwelling Spirit not to disappoint or fail.

What had been Christine's response? "See, you then?"

Layers of meaning in so few words.

Resting my forehead on the airplane window, I searched through the blanket of darkness for a sign. There was no angelic presence straddling the wing of the plane, smiling broadly, and giving me a thumbs up—no cloud formations spelling out the words that-a-boy. My physical eyes saw only darkness but I began to sense my inner vision begging to paint a different landscape. Trust was a muscle I had often neglected. Now, I understood that by letting trust support me, I could strengthen that muscle. I could see a trip filled with happy people.

The people of China rolled out their gracious welcome mat and we entered into the enchantment. We witnessed

117

the remarkable culture and explored firsthand the diversity of this historic terrain. We experienced the magical odyssey of 5000 years of recorded history in a vast and stunning landscape that beckoned us to stroll across its many wonders.

From the Forbidden City and Tiananmen Square, to the Ming Dynasty Tombs, meditating in Buddhist and Taoist temples, viewing the extraordinary Terracotta Warriors of Xian, cruising down Lake Kunming and the waterways of Shanghai, our senses were filled with joy and awe.

There was much to see and experience and we moved seamlessly as a group. Truly, Spirit never failed. In fact, Spirit soared! Reconnecting with trust was like a reunion with an old friend who had never left my side.

Each day, the group began with a prayer and mindfulness affirmation to center and focus us on all the things to celebrate in our lives.

With our guides Yin and Jinyuang, we gathered on the bus, merging both our physical presence and our cultural differences by staring in each other's eyes and praying:

> *Let all things be healthy.*
> *Let all things be peaceful.*
> *Be sure to count your blessings at least once a day.*
> *Forgive those who have hurt you,*
> *And those who have offended you.*
> *But first forgive yourself for what you have done,*
> *And what you have failed to do.*
> *That which is done there's no need to speak of,*

That which is past there's no need to blame.
Have self-control, self-knowledge, self-respect,
The courage to dare.
Be tranquil, the light of intelligence will shine.
Strive to make the spot where you stand beautiful.
Then the beauty and harmony will follow you in all your ways
And through all your days
On this splendid land of China. Amen.

The noise of excited conversation blended with the rhythmic thumping of the tires as the bus navigated the mountain. We were less than an hour outside of Beijing and there was reason for the heightened chatter—it was the day to visit and climb The Great Wall.

As we approached the entrance, clanging cymbals and music wafted through the windows of our bus. Vendors begged for our attention and the air was sweet smelling and thin from the altitude. Climbing The Great Wall was what I had looked forward to the most.

Before us lay massive steps that seemed to disappear into the clouds.

It was humbling to scale one of the greatest accomplishments of the ancient world, something that took millions of people through three dynasties to construct and was estimated to be over 6000 miles long. Stretching from the mountains of Korea to the Gobi Desert, it was still hard to imagine that radar images of this incredible structure could be detectable from space.

Exhilarated, I began climbing the uneven, steep steps.

There were times when I was thankful for the rail to hold onto. With knees burning, I kept going. I considered myself a decent hiker, but this was far more strenuous than expected. Undaunted, I advanced until a posted guard silently stood signaling that further climbing was unsafe due to crumbling stone.

I turned around. What a spectacular view! Only a panoramic camera could do this justice.

From this vantage point, I could barely make out the ant sized tour bus that belonged to my group. I marveled at the snake-like structure that had been my heavenly stairway as my lungs stung from the cool air.

Our guide explained that during the Qin Dynasty, China's first self-appointed emperor Shi Huang Ti, gave the order to start the wall's construction. It was initially designed to protect the empire from marauding tribes from the north. As a ruler, Shi Huang Ti abhorred deviation, fearing his empire would become unmanageable. He oversaw the burning of precious texts and the execution of many of his countries educators. During his rule, he sent countless tribes of free thinkers to work and often to die on his wall. Some estimates tell of more than a million people dying as laborers in one 3,000 mile section alone. The last thing our guide said was that the dead were simply buried among the brick and granite.

I stopped as these words echoed back in my thoughts. Humbled by my privileges, I ceremoniously rubbed the toe of my shoe through the mortared dust underfoot. More than just a wall, it was a tomb, housing the memories of ambition and longing of individuals that could well match my own. There was much to consider about the sacredness of life, as I stood high above the land.

Confucius once taught that every drop of water forms the ocean. Yet, is the ocean ever complete? Drops are consistently being added and evaporated. The people who gave their lives for this structure were drops in my ocean. Regardless of the centuries between us, their work and sacrifice were influencing this personal moment. Would this drop called David be of any measurable influence to someone else?

I began my descent, realizing this would take some time and careful calculation for the good of my knees.

About halfway down, I happened upon Angela and Christine. Yes, Christine was climbing! And, not just a little bit, she had made it further than most in our group. Angela wanted to climb to the top, and Christine asked if I would do the honors of escorting her back down.

"Certainly," I replied.

I counted each section of steps below us saying "high" or "low" according to their height. Our pace allowed us both to discover the carvings and inlaid stone that lined the interior. Running my finger across a circular indentation, I realized I had missed such things on my haste to ascend.

We took our time. Christine was unaware of the amazed looks of fellow climbers, who noticing her white cane, did double takes.

"Can you smell that?" she would ask and my eyes would search for the vendor roasting something indiscernible over coals. There, two landings and a considerable distance below us, sat an elderly Chinese man, his make shift grill emitting faint trails of scented smoke.

"Chestnuts?' I questioned.

"Nah," she said, "then I'd think I was in Rockefeller Plaza."

Switching senses, she announced, "sounds Portuguese," picking out one of the many varying languages that blanketed our ears.

Turning on a tape recorder looped around her fannypack, Christine documented every auditory stimulus from the bustling wind to the conversations of climbers made choppy by their breathing. She captured the music still discernible from our place of origin, a sort of mandolin and cymbals combo reminiscent of a John Philip Souza march. I didn't remember any of this on the way up. I must have zoned out, letting my legs do all the work. A flash of realization went through me. Christine was my escort, not the other way around. She was leading me through an entirely new, all-sensory experience, one where I was required to be fully present.

When I questioned her about the recording, she said it helped with her presentations.

"Presentations?" I asked.

"Yes, I often travel and then share my experiences with organizations for the disabled. It's my way of letting my audience know there's a whole world out there just waiting to be explored."

Lao Tse, the Chinese philosopher once taught, "If you

tell me, I will listen. If you show me, I will see. But, if you let me experience, I will learn."

Christine seemed more than just a drop in my ocean, she felt like a wave. Her influence came crashing into my awareness through telling, showing and experiencing life in a whole new way.

Why would a blind person want to go on a sightseeing tour? I think the more pertinent question is on the tour of life, why would we choose to close our eyes, our hearts to any part of the adventure? Why let fear override the greater possibility?

Robert Jacques Turgot, France's Minister of Finance under Louis the XVI once expressed, "What I admire in Columbus is not his having discovered a world but his having gone to search for it on the faith of an opinion."

To be in Christine's world, one must not only have faith in the opinion but faith in the discovery.

Her lens to this world is filtered through the description given by others. Yet, at no time did she seem to consider her life less because of it. In fact, her remaining physical senses aligned with an intuitive sense far more advanced than most.

On the bus that afternoon, no one complained of an ache or pain. I suspect it was because seated among us was someone who, without physical sight, had guided us to a higher place of human expression, a place where limitation has no hold, and we are free to climb the stars.

123

1) *What do you consider your greatest liability or limitation?*

2) *With closer examination, are you willing to explore the possibility that these considered limitations are selfimposed? If, as in the case of Christine, they are not self-imposed but a physical handicap, are you willing to see them as a gift, as a way to inspire others?*

3) *How do you feel about the statement, "Spirit never fails?"*

Sticks and Stones Support the Bones

It was my first holiday season as a minister in Religious Science. Standing in the entry way of the church where I was on staff, the pre-service silence was broken by the clatter of the metal mail slot opening and closing. A collection of varying sized envelopes and magazines resounded with a thud as they hit the tiled floor. I stopped my preparations for the mid week gathering and quickly glanced through the pile. There in bright Christmas red was an envelope addressed to me.

"A Christmas card!" I happily thought and eagerly opened it to see who it was from. Inside the envelope was not a traditional holiday card but an 8 X 5 index card accompanied by two photographs. The two images were of me. One was from a memorial I had facilitated several months earlier and the other from my recent installation ceremony with the church. The difference in the two pictures was my facial hair. I was sporting a goatee in the last one. The index card read something like, "Notice the sickly and inappropriate way you look with that stuff on your face. No respecting minister would stand in front of people with facial hair and expect us to believe them, much less be inspired by them." It was anonymously signed Enough Said.

I was stunned. It had been awhile since I was disarmed by the blatant absence of tact. My thoughts spiraled into adolescent reactiveness. I immediately wanted to drive to one of those warehouse grocery stores and buy the 24 pack of toilet paper, find the card senders address and "decorate" their yard. Better yet, why not call a pizza delivery service and order a half dozen of their most expensive pies delivered to their door—at midnight. I imagined the lovely correspondence Jesus might have received had this person attended one of his impromptu hillside gatherings.

It was hardly an edifying chain of thought. Yet, I justified allowing this mental steam to be blown in order to tame the potential destruction from a hibernating, unenlightened geyser of anger.

During the final weeks of the holiday season, I still found myself mentally obsessing over the note and permitting the seeming injustice to irritate and annoy me. Unaware of how much the disease to please was resting in my bones, I tossed and turned with the uncomfortable thought that somebody out there didn't approve or like me.

As December 31st approached, enough mental stability returned to encourage me to consider forgiving the mysterious pen pal. I knew I did not want to take this uneasy feeling into the new year. Big on ceremony, I created a burning bowl out of a conch shell from my private altar and placed the picture and the card inside. On my back porch at five minutes to midnight under a spectacular starry sky, I set them on fire, symbolizing my willingness to move beyond this emotional hurdle. Speaking my declaration of desire, I prayed, "Let me see the good in this."

The explosion of illegal bottle rockets and blaring car horns soon jolted the stillness of the neighborhood, as the countdown to another January was complete.

Breathing in the cool night air, I suddenly heard the question, "*How do you feel about the goatee?*"

"*I like it,*" I answered silently. It felt good to have a little variety in my appearance.

"*Then if you like it, shouldn't that be all that matters?*"

"*Well, of course, but it's never as simple as that,*" I argued.

"*Isn't it? You wish to be confident in your own choices, right? Then you might choose to see that card as an unexpected gift?*"

A gift? Now that was stretching it. How could something that felt so insulting be a gift? But some how the billowing smoke from the small fire seemed to carry away any fixated resistance. Leaning against the brick pillar on the porch, I finally smiled at this little dramatic episode. All that truly matters is how I feel about the facial hair. I like the way it looks. It's fun to groom and gives me a partial reprieve from the act of shaving.

What this person did was "give" me the opportunity to

look at how I feel about it and hold true to my personal convictions. Opinions come and go, but the true test of experiencing happiness is in remaining loyal to my own heart.

If my foundation is rocked by every derogatory comment then it's a foundation in need of serious repair. I had no idea mine was still so fragile. It was time to strengthen it—to fill the foundation of this new chapter in my life with equal parts appreciation and depersonalizing things.

I moved to the old wooden rocking chair under the patio awning and sat wrapped in my multi colored patchwork quilt. With eyes closed, I thought of why someone would create such correspondence in the first place—perhaps unhappy with their own life, the sight of my goatee setting off a bad memory, elderly and holding on to some antiquated opinion. I made a visual guess of their face and whispered thank you—thank you for helping me create a stronger foundation—thank you for helping me honor my own decisions. Suddenly this nondescript face softly laughed, winked at me and seemed to respond, *"Glad to be of service."*

My mind drifted as I gently rocked in the coolness of the late hour. This whole scenario was another wake up call to appreciation, that transmuting and transformative attribute of immeasurable power. It is easy to focus on the splinters of human drama that seem to bury themselves under our skin. Finding and focusing on the things to be grateful for invites the cosmic tweezer to come and bring about true relief.

I recalled playing the childhood game Deserted Island, reviewing in my mind how it was really a practice in appreciation. The rules ask you to imagine being a castaway. Your solace is that you get to choose the creature comforts that mean the most to you. For my food choice it would have to be the traditional American breakfast of eggs and hash browns; music—the vintage recordings of Dinah Washington and the idol from my 20s, Gino Vanelli; and books, well, that challenging decision would have to be narrowed down to my well-worn copy of the inspiring fable *The Journey Home*.

It is the story of Michael Thomas, a young man at the end of his wearisome rope. His name represents that dualistic struggle between the essence of The Archangel Michael and the fear-based energy of Thomas the Doubter. It is a challenge that many of us recognize—our spiritual nature going head to head with our old fear based beliefs. From a place of despair Michael Thomas decides he's "done" with the unpredictable fragility of this world. He feels as though he's drowning in personal disappointments and cries out his desire to simply "go home."

He gets his wish and winds up on an adventure which leads him to seven houses, each hosted by a grand angel. In these houses, individually corresponding to the seven colors of the chakras, he is taught attributes and insights by these unconditionally loving beings.

As I continued to rock in the wooden chair, I thought about Michael Thomas' visit to the house of relationships. The phenomenon of relating to others, with all its expectations, exhilarations and yes, even the blatant absence of tact— it all seemed less complex and mysterious through

129

the fable's premise. In the story, our protagonist certainly experiences his share of disappointment in romantic and familial love. With trepidation he leaves the traveled Oz-like path to enter this vibrant red house. The equally vibrant red angel greets him warmly at the front door and welcomes him inside. Escorted to a theatre style room, the angel instructs Michael Thomas to have a seat in front of a large movie screen. A slide show of people from his life begins to appear. The slides come alive and speak to him, telling him of their purpose in his life and the agreements that were made to facilitate evolutionary growth. Over the course of his years on earth, these agreements generated feelings that brought young Michael Thomas to his current crossroad.

There were pictures of family and inspirational teachers, the schoolyard bully and his real first love, but the slide that initiated immeasurable internal anger was of one particular woman. The face before him had been responsible for the death of his parents. Driving while intoxicated, she had swerved in front of his mom and dad's car and hit them head on. They were killed instantly. As all the previous slides had done, this one came to life and the woman softly spoke to Michael Thomas. She explained that her agreement had been to help him learn forgiveness so that he could be a powerful instructor of peace for others. As she smiled back at him alongside the contented faces of his parents, his heart softened and his feelings about the woman dramatically shifted.[3]

The lesson was about fulfilling contracts and becoming enlightened to the fact that at the most fundamental level, we all are one.

An unprecedented paradigm shift followed for me after reading this remarkable story. I had previously come to believe that in some way the people that we interact with and meet in our human lives are all a part of a collective soul group. Yet I never fully explored this idea of soul agreements. At the time it felt revolutionary, but strangely sensible, to imagine large groups gathering together before entering this earthly realm. Going around the vast circle of souls, it seemed logical for everyone to request what life lessons they would like to improve upon in this next incarnation. Some ask to be healed of bigotry, intolerance or the dance with self-doubt. Some request abandonment or abuse to be the catalyst for their spiritual odyssey. Others say all of the above plus the opportunity to fully embrace and master forgiveness.

"What had I asked for?" I wondered. Certainly all of the things listed above woven with an intense longing to feel a personal connection to God.

And then the thought occurred to me. *What if the most notorious perpetrators of grief and sorrow in our lives were actually the ones who loved us the most?* If we accept the idea that those we encounter are a part of this soul collective—that we come into this lifetime with agreements to fulfill, then perhaps it is those who love and honor us beyond measure that volunteer to bring these gifts to us expeditiously. We asked for expansion in self-esteem. They stood in that etheric circle, smiled and said, "I love you so much. I want you to have the desires of your heart. Let me come down and play

131

the role of the person who causes you the most grief in the area of self-love. This will create an explosion of longing within you so profound that you become diligent in your quest to capture it."

"The only catch," they add, "is that my vibration will be reduced to such a low frequency to fulfill this role that I will forget who I am. Your mastery in self-love can assist both of us in shedding light on the darkened pain and carry us back to a place of remembering.

It was a radical shift in my consciousness. Could I actually review the people from my past and see the perfection in all of the events surrounding my relationship to them? Could I remember on some basic, organic level that it was all just agreements between loving souls? Just as the mental image of the pseudo Christmas card sender had winked at me, I started going through the itinerary of those that had "done me wrong" and visualized them winking as well. Their grins widen to full on smiles as they tell me how proud they are that I'm able to see the truth in the dynamics of our interrelating—that I am starting to remember.

Joan Borysenko, in her book *Inner Peace for Busy People*, explains the work of Dr. Daniel Amen, a psychiatrist who studies how brain chemistry affects behavior. He calls it the 18/40/60 rule. At 18, you care very much what other people think of you; at 40, you don't give a damn what they're thinking; and at 60, you realize that no one was thinking about you anyway. Borysenko suggests that we are not the center of other people's universes. "Their role is not to judge, nor ours to obey. Inner peace requires us to develop the authority to direct our own lives, and the respect to allow other people to live theirs."[4] This viewpoint suggests that the energy we expend in defending ourselves against those who are "out to get us," or the mental laboring over past encounters with emotional firing squads might qualify as misunderstandings of our imagination. Simply put, we've forgotten who we are. But, as real as our hurdles may seem, we are still encouraged to give thanks for being taught to stretch our legs and jump.

I once had the privilege to sit and talk with a gentleman who seemed to have mastered the art of detaching from the supposed judgments of his past. As a child, he was challenged with severe dyslexia. Those years of his adolescence corresponded with an era where not much was known or understood about this disorder. He was demoted to special education classes and labeled as a problem student—unsuited for academia. His days in classrooms were filled with the shame of being laughed at. Unable to read the simplest word, he was often chided by student and teacher alike with the question, "What's wrong with you? Are you stupid?"

But a compassionate counselor took note of his accelerated IQ test scores and knew there must be more to him than his inability to read at an accepted level. "Life is a bell curve," the counselor shared. "Let the good parts play big brother to the ungainly and let the shortcomings be wise enough to tag along." He was asked to let this challenge be a springboard to his greatness.

An opthomolgist helped pinpoint the problem and his

133

life began to turn around. He channeled his anger at being ridiculed into what he called heightened coping skills. In hindsight, he gives thanks for dyslexia and the taunting he endured. It propelled him to gain clarity in his vision with an intent and determination that seemed indestructible. Now, a highly respected psychotherapist, his ability to visually and auditorally "hear" his clients creates a compassionate approach in the multi-dimensional perspective of their healing. He recognized that it was the counselor **and** the name callers that facilitated his personal growth. Rather than viewing his journey as cursed, he sees it as an indispensable gift.

With Gratitude as our Intention we become Fully Transformed (GIFT). This simple acronym helps motivate me to move into the awareness that things are not always as they seem. The birth of the gift is there if I choose to receive it, if I am willing to cut up my membership card to Club Blame. This gratitude, understanding and forgiveness, as reiterated earlier in the book, is not a call to passivity. It is not door mat consciousness. As Marianne Williamson used to comment, "Forgiving and honoring our past perpetrators does not mean we have to have lunch with them." Getting clear on the lesson and accepting the "gift" of their presence does not require us to stick around and subject ourselves to more abuse. Appreciate the lesson and move on.

Time and time again, history shows that adversity plays mid-wife to many of our greatest accomplishments. The pain from our youth drove us away from the limited nest and in so doing, we discovered our wings. The longing for living a life with purpose becomes more important than the familiarity of our misery—or as Shirley MacLaine once inspired, "In order to get to the fruit of the tree, you have to go out on a limb."

We are invited to shift our beliefs about the painful events of our past and climb out on that radical limb where the fruit of sweet freedom awaits to be tasted. Instead of chanting the playground song of "sticks and stones may break my bones" we sing out the new, enlightened version of the lyric "sticks and stones *support* the bones."

As Neal Donald Walsch writes in *Conversations With God, Book 2*, "I tell you this: every person who has ever come to you has come to receive a gift from you. In so doing, they give a gift to you—the gift of your experiencing and fulfilling who you are. When you see this simple truth, when you understand it, you see the greatest truth of all: *I have sent you nothing but angels.*"[5]

Consequently, we transform our opinions about all our relationships. No longer are some labeled as detestable weeds in our life's garden but we pay homage to the willing thought that all were useful flowers adorning our history's landscape.

The more we ready ourselves to adopting this viewpoint the less it is necessary to create some painful interaction for the contractual lessons. By transcending thoughts of victimization and entertaining the idea of a perfect journey, we master the lessons we said we wanted in that etheric, cosmic circle. We can choose to move forward on our path of purpose with greater joy. Our deepening awakens a clarity and awareness within that makes the events of this human world seem less traumatic and negatively charged—more kind and infinitely more loving.

In the reflective hour of that winter night, I glimpsed a slight fraction of what it might be like to possess the senses of God: to see the totality of the world as one big ongoing passion play where all the characters shine with the light of truth; to reason with a wisdom that knows no limitation and understands that all souls are created equal—to touch, taste, and hear only love—without reservation, knowing that God cannot lie, God cannot hate—God sees all as holy creations.

Being willing to have my senses influenced by the senses of God seemed a liberating resolution. Funny how one single envelope helped usher in a very happy New Year.

1) *Make a list of those whom you would consider to be your biggest perpetrators of grief and pain.*

2) *With a sense of willingness, consider that their participation in your life was a contract, an agreement to help you grow in this lifetime. How does the possibility of this concept make you feel?*

3) *GIFT = with Gratitude as our Intention we become Fully Transformed. This transformation enters our life experience as paradigm shifts occur in our beliefs about relationships, work, health, etc. What area of your life would you welcome a shift in consciousness? By using the acronym as a formula for change, you'll see that finding gratitude (the gift) in everything will bring about this desired shift.*

Come Down From the Tree

As the motorcade for my sister Becky's funeral made its way toward the grave site ceremony, it hadn't occurred to me that we would actually pass through my childhood neighborhood. The procession of cars, traveling by way of the main thoroughfare through Beaumont, intersected the very road where I lived and played as a boy—Abilene Ave.

Creeping along, escorted by dual motorcycle cops, our speed was such that I could get a good, long look at the house, the street, and the yard where I grew up. Still thriving at the edge of the lawn by the ditch was the mimosa tree. That tree, with its bountiful pink blossoms, the one my mother kept threatening to have cut down because of the mess it made of the yard, that glorious tree was my haven. The way mimosa trees grow, the branches arch up and grow out, leaving hollow pockets in which a boy can hide from

139

the world. In this elevated sanctuary of limbs and dense green foliage, I could pretend that the abuse and the yelling in the flat-topped house below belonged to another family.

I turned, staring out the rear window of the hearse, trying to keep the tree in my field of vision for as long as possible. Everyone riding with me assumed I was looking at our old house, but my eyes held fast to the tree until finally, it disappeared from sight.

Disappeared visually perhaps, but the door of my mind was now flung open to some of the most vivid memories and private moments of my life.

Every summer, the Tyrell Public Library had a contest for the student who read the most books during school break. And, in September, in front of a new teacher, a representative from the library would come and personally give out certificates with shiny gold foiled emblems pasted on. I was the lucky recipient several times, but I would have been just as pleased to give the library an award. Their opened doors ushered me into a world of words that became my salvation.

I developed a fondness for biographies and worked my way through a particular group designed for young readers.

So, with the stories of Abraham Lincoln, Walt Disney, Abner Doubleday, Harriet Tubman or George Washington Carver among others, tucked under my arm, I'd climb the trunk of that mimosa tree and settle in. The branches draped and sheltered me from the world as I became transported into theirs. My reading, mixed with daydreams and wanderlust, made me wonder if my life would ever evolve into anything as significant as the life stories I held in my hands.

Somewhere around the age of eight, I calculated how many years were left before I could legally leave home and placed corresponding thumbtacks for each of those years into the bark of the mimosa. It was an act signifying my Marco Polo phase. Just as the famous Venetian explorer left markers to help him navigate, I fashioned my thumbtacks in the shape of an arrow, pointing me toward an illusive future. The little metal dots were my visual to hang in there, believing my time would come. It was vital to preserve my instinct to explore. The stories I read encouraged the desire for trail-blazing, and I was destined to move far beyond those branches, this town. Every birthday, I'd take a penny or dime and pry out one of the now rusted thumbtacks, imagining the day when that makeshift metal arrow was reduced to one tiny dot on a map of bark. Next to it, I would carve the phrase "you were here," appreciating the significance of the past tense.

The beautiful thing of reading about the lives of those famous people was the spark of recognition that occurred. Up in that tree, I often thought, "If they can do it, so can I." If these inventors, statesmen, geniuses, and freedom fighters could move over every conceivable hurdle, then why not me?

That sense of "why not me" made my heart swell with possibilities. No obstacle seemed too great. I was willing to invest my hope in the freedom of the mystery.

But, at the end of the day, I'd have to climb down from

those branches and enter the home-front ambush. My oldest brother, irrepressibly and psychologically damaged by our father's death, displayed an uncontrollable rage. He threatened and chased the rest of us; the supposed safety of a closed door shattered by the force of his fist splintering the thin wood. Our faces were often smashed into the earth and sod with an order from him to "eat grass." And once, because age and size were on his side, he had lifted me above his head and hurled me into a wall. I bit my tongue so deep on impact that stitches seemed the only thing holding it together. It was not a good time.

Down on the ground, away from my protective tree, I longed to twitch my nose and disappear like Samantha, on the television show Bewitched. But, there seemed nowhere to go. My heart began flip-flopping from the inspiration of "why not me" to the desolate resolve of "why me."

How many of us still live in that "why me" mentality even after we're long removed from the physical situations that birthed it? "Why me's" are like barnacles, clinging to the walls of our sunken belief systems—parasitic memories eating at us and blocking the progression of living with infinite possibility. Yet, many of us forget that their presence is optional. We simply accept the burdensome weight of their energy as an unavoidable travel companion. "Why me's" create that frequent sense of futility and help formulate the mantra that "this is as good as it gets."

It's easy to spot a "why me" belief system in operation. For starters, it feeds and supports a personal manifesto that reads, "Because of the mistakes of my past, I am destined for failure. There is no escape." It stirs up stale excuses—ingredients in a vast soup pot we call our mismanaged lives. Unconsciously, we serve these thoughts to the world as representative of who we are. Is it really any great wonder, then, that the self-fulfilling prophecy kicks in? The world spits the "why me" believer back out, eliciting sighs about no respect, no love, no demonstration.

"Why me" lets our blood relatives dictate our choices long after we've left their physical presence. "Why me" operators also get the most upset when others exhibit any kind of deepening or growth. That in-your-face expansion threatens their status quo. They are the ones who will complain about their situation, their health, their job, their marriage, and their finances, yet will slam the door shut when growth opportunities appear.

I once counseled a young man who struggled with acquiring and maintaining a job. His dyslexia created terror within him whenever it came time to fill out a job application. He didn't have the money to purchase a car and depended on his grandmother for transportation. He rarely took the time to groom or bathe himself. His nearly undetectable self-esteem would rise and fall according to whether or not this one particular girl he had met online responded to him. His one solution for happiness, to have this girl, who lived clear across the country, agree to come and set up house. To him, it was not unusual that he had no job, no developed skills, no place to call his own, that he had created a false profile for his cyber love—if she showed up at

143

his door, then life would be worth living.

I explained the power and necessity of integrity and gave the *you can't live on love alone* counsel, relaying the ethical options of supporting ones self before ever attempting to support a relationship.

However, my heart went out to him. His desperate need for acceptance and love was clouding his choices in building a solid foundation for his life. I offered to work with him for free, create a resume targeting his strengths, and make phone calls to potential employers.

But, it was all too threatening. He didn't want to let go of the "life is hard" synopsis scripted by "why me." After the offers, I never saw him again.

Now the humbling part—every time I observe that behavior in another, I have to wake up to the sobering fact that I'm looking in a mirror, that there is still a bit of "why me" within myself.

Ernest Holmes, author and founder of Religious Science wrote, "This original life is infinite. It is good. It is filled with peace. It is of the essence of purity. It is the ultimate of intelligence. It is power. It is Law. It is Life. It is in us. In that inner sanctuary of our nature, hidden perhaps from objective gaze, nestles the seed, perfection."[6]

The world continues to wait patiently for our big idea to merge with that sense of perfection. Combining these two creates the ripple of positive change that spreads throughout our life and the world.

In Religious Science teaching, we often toss around the phrase "principle is not bound by precedent." Simply put, your past does not define who you are. Your diagnosis does not shut the door to the possibility for wholeness, for you are far greater than the limitations dictated within the framework of your physical body. Your history of disappointing relationships does not govern or deny your right to deserve love and compassion. Your financial challenge is not representative of a greater life force at work against you. All these familiar limitations are like birds in a doorless cage. Giving up the "why me" energy illuminates the exit sign and points us to freedom. But, walking around, whispering, repeating and giving energy to the belief in "why me" circumvents any substantial growth in these areas. It muddies our conscious windshield and distorts the truth of what lies ahead. "Why me" equals playing small. "Why not me" joins with the unlimited possibilities that help guide us to our power and purpose.

When you see success around you, look at the beauty of it, the intricate detail in which it was brought to form and bless it. As you bless it, say to yourself, "why not me?" Why not invite in the same ingredients for the success you observe into your own experience? When you see optimum health, look at that wholeness and vibrancy and repeat, "why not me." That experience is your birthright.

When you notice couples holding hands or observe the kind of affection you secretly long for, do you roll your eyes in judgment, yet ache inside for the same? If so, try repeating "why not me" at each observation of connubial bliss. For every moment you choose a "why not me" experience, you break away from your limited history or negative family influence. What you do with that experience determines the gifts you get from the Universe.

Vibrating with a "why not me" mantra restores us to the purity of eagerness, that eagerness that thrived before the intervening disappointments watered down its potency.

I opted to fly on an economy airline to Salt Lake City recently. You know the one, no first class, no meals, just pretzels and a first-come-first-served seating arrangement. So, you can imagine my surprise, after taking my place on an aisle seat, to look across and see Dick Clark in the aisle seat across from me. Next to him sat his wife. When our eyes met, he smiled that uncomfortable, acknowledging smile that seemed to say, "Hello, I see you there, but please don't engage me in conversation. Let me fly in peace."

I could respect that. The young woman next to me, however, could not. Her youth was accented with a midriff top that showed her perfectly flat stomach with the accompanying belly button piercing. Her blond highlights were symmetrically running through her already blonde hair and she topped off the look with perfect nails and big platform shoes. Everything seemed to call out—actress. Our young passenger saw Mr. Clark at the same time I did and let out a semi contained gasp. She began to fidget in her seat, asking those around us if they had anything to write on. Unsuccessful, her request turned to obtaining a pen and someone finally passed one from the row behind. She then frantically searched through the seat pocket in front of her, retrieving the nausea bag. On it, the starry-eyed actress to famous producer correspondence began. Seated so close, I couldn't help eavesdropping and reading what she was writing. She was creating an impromptu letter and resume on this nausea bag.

"You've got to be kidding me," I cynically thought. *"Nothing is going to come from that. Stop wasting your time, his time, and practice some preventive restraint with your fragile hope."*

Wow. Where did that come from? Was some buried cynicism from an unfulfilled part of my own acting career rising up to wreak its havoc on all show biz possibilities? It was definitely time to defuse the toxic mind chatter. That's the great thing about committing to a spiritual, conscious path. I catch myself faster. Now, as I resolved to appreciate this young girl and acknowledge her eagerness, she leaned over to me and asked, "How do you spell incur?"

The question became the official "invitation" in helping and sharing her mission.

I quickly retrieved my own nausea bag and began helping her compose a witty, memorable and correctly spelled letter to the famous producer. Her pure eagerness became contagious, exciting, and I found myself taking the essence of that eagerness and transforming my own experience. I was given this humorous scenario to look at how life presents us with innumerable opportunities. How quickly do we judge them as impossible based on our history? How quickly do we cancel out pursuing an opportunity for fear of looking foolish? This wonderful teacher, sitting next to me, would have none of that. She was diving headfirst into an ocean of "why not me" possibilities.

After we landed, we agreed that she should present it to him once we were walking in the terminal. Running awkwardly in her platform shoes, she gave Mr. Clark our composition. From my vantage point, I could see him graciously laugh, shake her hand and introduce her to his wife. Her mission in that moment was fulfilled. However, I was feeling strangely incomplete with the whole thing. Picking up my pace to reach them, the girl departed and I found myself in stride with this American icon. "I proofread that!" I mused, out of the corner of my mouth, causing both he and his wife to laugh even harder. I turned a corner and leaned against the airport wall, laughing myself at the childlike exuberance I was feeling. It was another conscious turning point in committing to a deeper walk with "why not me." God bless the actress.

As safe as I felt in the branches of that mimosa tree, the years have revealed the necessity for me to come down and participate in life. Yet, just because my physical body made the journey to terra firma, certain emotional parts of me remained guarded and hidden in an illusory nest high above. A number of my "why not me" beliefs were still tucked away there. Up in that tree, there was no need to conform. Down below, everything felt controlled by constant negotiation. Now, more than ever, I longed to integrate the imaginative dreams of my childhood into the neglected parts of the adult David—the areas that still felt too painful to acknowledge. Sometime before my teens, I abandoned the conviction in the dreams that had whispered to me from the pages of those autobiographies. My immediate world seemed to say, "Forget about it," and at times, I felt tempted to do so. Yet, the Lincoln's and Tubman's of the world had not forgotten, and so I would not allow myself to fully disengage from all hope. In my adult years, the irony was that I went about creating opportunities for myself with almost reckless abandon—advancing my education, writing and producing my own material as an actor, writing and producing my own music. I could never sit around and wait for something to happen. I had to get in there and create it for myself. Although this approach does not seem to fit the profile of someone emotionally clinging to memories in a tree, I could objectively see that in all those endeavors, I believed in the struggle. I appeared to be a "why not me" spirit on the outside, wearing the appropriately labeled sash for all to see, but my internal allegiance was far more compatible with the futile alternative. My convictions fell into alignment with exertion and efforting, not with the beauty of simply creating. Again, feeding the "why me" monster inside.

We must all come down from the tree. But, we are invited to bring down with us the belief in the possible and integrate it into our human experience. The world needs us to look beyond the eyes of the ambush and diffuse its influence. With enough eager hearts shouting "why not me," we can contribute to the healing of the planet on a significant scale.

I love the paradoxical commandments written by Kent Keith. This list of principles, an assignment Keith had writ-

149

ten for a class at Harvard in the 1960s, had unknowingly made its way around the world. Some thirty years later, it graced the walls of Shishu Bhavan, the children's home in Calcutta, which was run by Mother Teresa. Of the ten timeless principles, one of my favorites reads, "The biggest men and women with the biggest ideas can be shot down by the smallest men and women with the smallest minds. Think big anyway."

The life stories that inspired me as a young boy were filled with decisions to think big in spite of overpowering odds. Thinking big anyway is synonymous with choosing a "why not me" attitude.

Now, when I allow myself to objectively view the choice between the futile and the infinite, the choice becomes eagerly obvious.

1) With the tree as metaphor for our imagination, we rest high above in its infinite branches, cradled by the support of Spirit. There we entertain the ideas of greatness and weave our dreams that know no boundaries. List some of your "why not me" inspirations.

2) The chapter shows three distinct realities; the tree (imagination), the books (inspiration and guidance) and the earth plain (the human experience). Can you recall a time when these realities appeared incongruent in your life? What race conscious beliefs of "why me" settled in as a result?

3) What "why not me" ideas seem retrievable, even after years of neglect, doubt and fear?

Taming the Tempo

Just thinking about Jack makes me tired. He's running up hills to fetch pails of water. He's trying his best to be nimble and quick while hurdling over burning candles. To cap it all off, the poor guy has to work extra hard to support his spouse's eating habit—a woman who can eat no lean.

Everything about this nursery rhyme legend suggests that Jack's life has somehow evolved into a series of unmanageable circumstances.

For many, this unmanageability is more than just an annoying problem. It has emerged as a full-fledged epidemic.

Recovering that sense of balance between work and rest seems ripe for discussion by nearly every inspirational author, lecturer, minister and counselor I hear today. Taming our "to do" list animal has become a critical priority, as many of us experience a breakdown in our physical lives—

153

the "Jack" within all of us tumbling and crashing down
that overscheduled hill.

We function in society with an undercurrent of urgency
that buzzes like an artificial light, a switch constantly flipped
to the on position. Whether we realize it or not, this high
voltage beam shines on the underlying notion that there is
not enough—not enough time, not enough resources, not
enough love. We work harder to merely maintain, fulfilling
the observation of Frank Lloyd Wright that we become "little
more than janitors of our possessions."

At no time was this problem more glaringly brought to
my attention than over the 2001 holiday season. As I lay in
the hospital during the weeks spanning Christmas and
New Year, I came to the realization that I had not allowed
myself to "stop" in nearly 15 years. That youthful feeling of
invincibility I assumed would prevail forever had come to a
screeching halt. I unwittingly reserved my space next to
Jack at the bottom of that hill, a place littered with broken
and exhausted souls feeling anything but invincible. The
saga of the lingering cough joined forces with innumerable
other complications, leaving me hooked to and monitored
by machines for weeks—electrocardiograms, a bronchos-
copy, an endoscopy, asthma testing. Even brain scans were
intermingled with tube feeding to help counter my immense
weight loss. My adrenal system had completely shut down
and my kidneys, liver, and spleen sluggishly tried to function. Other than my birth, I had never been admitted in the
hospital. The required surrender was immensely foreign
yet welcomed as those first few days blurred together with

procedure after procedure and a fatigue-induced sleep so deep that it took on fairy-tale proportions. As thankful as I was at each benign biopsy or negative test result, I couldn't help but wonder what was really going on internally for me to create such dramatic health challenges. Had my inability to stop become so all pervasive that a force greater than me had to step in to assist? I was scared. As ridiculous as it sounds, I felt I could deal with the situation easier if there were a diagnosis. I could wrap my mind around something like the suspected cancer and begin to work with the specifics in getting better. Continuing to look for the next thing, going through the medical process of elimination, made the mystery seem all the more ominous.

Lying in that hospital bed late one evening, I took the comment card from the adjacent dresser drawer and began to fill it with my own comments to God:

I feel a weariness that goes beyond physical exertion. It is like a secret bucket, hidden from the world, and continuing to fill up with my private tears. The weight of responsibility collects, and the tears slosh around so that each step becomes increasingly labored. Eventually this bucket spills over into the outward expression of crying but that does little to empty out the unbearable weight—the weight of sorrows, regrets, and unexpressed disappointments. I guess there has to be a collapse—an earthquake of the soul that takes that bucket and completely flips it over. It makes for a messy, emotional display. No matter how great the longing to keep it all together, there is a greater requirement to sur-

155

render and embrace that collapse.

I feel like I don't know anything anymore. I don't understand the cough or its presence in my life. I'm so far "in it" that I can't even see which direction to extend my hands for help. So, I'm flailing in the dark and grasping at a collection of straws that hold no answers. I don't know what to do other than to continue to explore and wait, explore and wait. I feel uncertain as to what I'm supposed to pursue now or how I'm to conquer the cycle of debt that has surfaced from all this. For the first time in a great while, I am consumed by indescribable loneliness.

So, I ask for help. If 2001 was the cyclone, then I pray that the new year will be the relief effort to help clean it all up. I've somehow disconnected from my intuition, your guidance and placed all my faith in only what the physical world is presenting me. I need to find my authentic voice again—the one that cannot be silenced by all of this nonsense.

Dare I say that I choose to be happy with my life, every unexpected detour, because the alternative hasn't been very appealing? I need to learn how to say no and not obsess over whether or not I've disappointed someone.

My thoughts are far from unique. As I travel and speak about recovering the necessary balance in our lives, people tend to sigh with a teary weariness, expressing their doubt in really finding a personal solution. We often lament, "If I can just make this deadline, get through this year, get this child through graduation, then I can schedule some time for me." Yet, the to-do lists are never complete, and the deadlines are always followed by more, fueling and spinning the proverbial hamster wheel of activity.

As a child, I did not know any better than to accompany my bicycling friends behind the DDT truck as it drove through our neighborhood spraying for mosquitoes. Chasing the poison mist that exploded from the giant sprayer was part of our summer ritual. The one who could stand the stinging eyes and lungs the longest was declared the winner. Today, I would never do such a thing. I've grown wise to such foolhardy dangers and would appropriately remove myself from the vicinity of any poison. Yet, we don't have the wherewithal to remove ourselves from the "poison" of over doing. Many of us still ride into the fog as if it were a contest, the prize, our ability to endure the longest.

Perhaps no one has addressed this topic of imbalance more brilliantly than Wayne Muller in his ground breaking book *Sabbath*. Muller reminds us that what we are missing is our connection with Sabbath. Sabbath is more than an antiquated idea that requires us to observe our religious convictions on a particular calendar day, it is offered as a way of life. "Sabbath is more than the absence of work. It is time consecrated with our attention, our mindfulness, honoring those quiet forces of grace or spirit that sustain and heal us. To practice Sabbath is to remember and honor this balance in the most sacred and personal way."[7] Every living thing was designed to operate within a natural rhythm of activity and rest. For every inhale, there follows an exhale. For every blossoming season there is the stark stillness of winter. All of nature participates in this ebb and flow without question or strain except for one—human beings. Humans have the supreme ability to reason and choose, the highest form of wisdom on the evolutionary chain, yet can lack the insight to honor this sacred tempo.

We just keep going, equating action and accomplishment with success, never honoring ourselves for the wisdom in napping, watching a sunset or playing with a child. Somehow, being still is inappropriately linked to being lazy. We could learn a thing or two from the family dog. Chances are, Spike isn't worrying about his reputation when rolling over to let the morning sun warm his belly. Yet, we struggle in allowing ourselves to stop. We must keep up for our family's sake, for our careers. Regardless of the reminders to slow down or face the consequences, the merry-go-round remains full to capacity —the message lost in the deafening whirl of wind and noise. So why do we refuse to listen even when we know better? For one, there's something immensely scary when we are asked to focus on our feelings rather than the energy expended to avoid them. Muller uses the example of skipping stones across a pond. We are taught that the successful stone skipper hurls the rock at great speed, the goal to send the stone traveling as far as possible. What happens if we toss the rock too slowly? It disappears into a murky unknown. Most of us feel that if we stop hurling ourselves as fast as we can into life that we will somehow disappear. We would have to drop down to the core of our feelings where our orphaned vulnerabilities lay waiting to be visited.

We don't disappear. We actually come face to face with our power and the guidance in how to use it. All one can ask in order to get us to see that is implore us to trust enough in the unfamiliar journey and embrace the places that scare us. Just as my ride with sorrow, in the beginning of the book, propelled me to a greater place of freedom and healing, so does visiting the silence introduce us to the answers we've longed for.

My greatest realization from the imposed stillness of that hospital bed came from the last line in that comment card—my inability to say no. The truth of that simple awareness felt astonishing to me. Funny what a cyclone could distract me from. With wanting to be accepted and liked so deeply rooted, my saying yes was on automatic pilot. The affirmative was out of my mouth before I even had a chance to think about it. I was accustomed to doing whatever it took to create happy environments, happy people even at the expense of my own welfare. Many times, I boarded planes with a soaring fever or cold because I could not fathom calling and canceling an event. "Everyone's depending on me," I reasoned and so I must do my part to save the planet from misery and despair. All I needed to go with that idea was an old fashioned phone booth to change into my special cape of enlightenment.

All the energy that it takes to be the dutiful son, the responsible daughter, the uncomplaining employee, the understanding spouse or well providing parent must be balanced by the ability to recognize our needs and be willing to respect ourselves enough to ask for support. But with

159

a history of any kind of abuse comes a history of not being able to set boundaries. Oprah Winfrey made the comment that once your personal boundaries have been violated as a child, it's difficult to regain the courage to stop people from stepping on you. You fear being rejected for who you really are. She spent the first four decades of her life giving everything she could to almost anyone who asked, running herself ragged trying to fulfill other people's expectations of what she should do and who she should be.

Canceling my engagements during this time had upset a number of people. Knowing they were upset, yet not being able to do anything about it, was uncomfortable at best. There loomed within my consciousness the belief that an automatic yes response would keep any disharmony, chaos, or abuse at bay. Saying no was equated with being difficult, stingy, and chancing not being liked. I must have believed that being liked was far more important than taking care of myself.

As I listened to the night nurse try desperately to calm an angry patient next door, another insight came barreling towards me. *We can never please all of the people all of the time.* No matter how great the effort or how honorable the sacrifice, there will be those who will find fault with us regardless.

These two concepts, learning to say no and understanding that I will never be able to please everyone became like bookends for my brain. It did not mean that I was to stop striving for excellence. It simply meant that I needed to re-examine my intentions behind my commitments. What was

I doing it for?

The fluorescent lighting of that hospital room shone on more than just my arms so nurses could check my IV or for doctor's to write in my chart. It somehow illumined within me the importance of placing these bookends on the shelf of my day to day decision making process. Practicing the boundaries contained within this wisdom might keep me from ever having to visit here again.

During the next year I simply began to live with the fact that I was a decent, kind, and giving person—whether I responded to the world's request with a yes or a no. I could honor my mental checklist. Does what is being asked of me feel in line with being true to myself? Does saying yes resound within every fiber of my being—if not, what needs to be changed? As Oprah concluded, "You don't know what a genuine yes feels like if you're used to saying yes to everything. When it's right, your whole body feels it."[8]

With a great many of us identifying with nursery rhyme Jack's overwhelm, it becomes apparent that a change is needed. In order to lift ourselves out of the battered collection of bodies that populate the base of that hill, we must choose a different experience. As much as we want to complicate it, it really is that simple. You are enough, period. There's nothing you may have done that is so unforgivable that it requires you to spend the rest of your life making up for it. Stop. Accept the divinity of who you are and know that you can now start to nurture your greatness, the precious and unique gift of you. By inviting this truth to erase and replace any other label we may have given ourselves,

161

the energy expended becomes focused on the things that really matter. You can say no and feel OK about it.

Not only did this re-examination of my responses liberate me emotionally, it liberated me physically as I began to chart a course towards wholeness that I had never fully known before.

Taming the tempo of our lives isn't so much about exerting power over the unmanageable aspects of our immediate world, it's more about quieting our minds enough to hear our true voice and speaking its wisdom from a self-nurturing heart.

1) *There are so many small steps we can take to help bring about a more peaceful coexistence between our work life and our time for rest. What one taming practice could you implement today to help balance your own tempo?*

2) *Is saying no difficult for you? If so, what are your fears associated with that response?*

3) *Can you truthfully say that you honor your rest and quiet time as much as you honor your personal accomplishments and hourly actions? Do you view them as equally important? List the benefits of rest. Are these qualities that you desire for yourself?*

Epilogue

It has been just over a year and a half since the words of that first chapter came flooding out of me. The desire for this book felt fueled by an energy and a commitment never before experienced, as if the bolt on a gate was removed and a captive animal set free.

I rewrote a lot. I doubted my capabilities a lot. There were times when I questioned whether or not this book was even necessary. Yet, within me, the animal of expression pranced and ran and kicked with such presence and fortitude that I had to keep going.

In *The Hero with a Thousand Faces,* Joseph Campbell writes, "While all stories have already been told, this is not a bad thing since the retelling is still necessary."

I choose to believe that my storytelling is somehow necessary. With the inspiration I received from that beautiful sentence, I continually took off my critic's cap and put it away, trusting that, if anything, the words would be cathartic and healing for me.

And now I pray, healing for you, the reader. It is my intention that within these pages you've discovered the permission to embrace your own declarations of desire and purpose and allow yourself to move in the direction of their fulfillment.

The urgency of our days quiets to the trill of the mockingbird. The ache within our hearts is massaged and any remaining feelings of regret are cradled in the arms of simple grace. We can now look at the story of our own life and see the perfection in each step, each decision, honoring the fact that every choice got us to this present moment in time. We continue to evolve. At some profound moment, nestled in the awareness of our days, we discover that we will continue this path of deepening and learning for the rest of our lives.

I get that now. I see that these personal convictions are only representative of the middle of my story and that the road ahead is a welcoming one, if I choose to see it that way.

My windshield is repaired now, my vision that much clearer and I can appreciate the panorama of possibilities before me.

There are many that have gone along for the ride. I would like to express my sincere thanks to Maureen Hoyt for her editing skills and for supporting me so faithfully in this endeavor. Also thank you to Ann Townsend for additional proofreading, and to Jeff Dannels for creating the visual for me to see my book in print for the first time. To all those wonderful souls who attended the Wednesday night services at Granada Hills Church of Religious Science, thank you for providing a safe and loving forum in which to share these insights over the years.

Blessed be.

David Ault
December 2002

Sources and Permissions

Every effort has been made to trace copyright holders of material in this book. May your inspirations continue to live on.

Page 8: translations by Coleman Barks with John Moyne, The Essential Rumi, New York: Harper Collins Publishers, Inc., 1995

Page 16: Wayne Muller, How Then Shall We Live, New York: Bantam Books, Inc., 1996

Page 130: Lee Carroll, The Journey Home, Carlsbad, CA: Hay House, Inc., 1997. Used by permission of the author.

Page 133: Joan Borysenko, Inner Peace for Busy People: 52 Simple Strategies For Transforming Your Life, Carlsbad, CA: Hay House, Inc., 2001

Page 135: Neale Donald Walsch, Conversations With God, Book 2, Charlottesville, VA: Hampton Roads Publishing Company, Inc., 1997

Page 144: Ernest Holmes, The Science of Mind, New York: Jeremy P. Tarcher/Putnam, 1998 Originally published, New York: R. M. McBride and Company, 1938

Page 157: Wayne Muller, Sabbath: Finding Rest, Renewal, and Delight in our Busy Lives, New York: Bantam Books, Inc. 1999

Page 161: Oprah Winfrey, The Oprah Magazine, Volume 1, Number 2, New York: Hearst Communications, Inc. July/August 2000

For a complete listing of products and
services by David Ault and The Conscious
Company, please visit www.DavidAult.com
or www.ConsciousCo.com.

Or write: The Conscious Company
P.O. Box 931418
Los Angeles, CA 90093-1418